Praise for **Moms Mean Business**

"**Moms Mean Business** is a must-read book for aspiring and established mom entrepreneurs. Not only does it give you the nuts and bolts for running a successful business, but it also provides an individualized approach that includes nurturing your personal life alongside your business life."

—Holly Hanna, Work at Home Woman

"Reading this book is like having your very own mentor. Women seeking advice on getting started or growing their business can find real guidance, with real plans and real inspiration. It's like being able to pick the brains of fellow moms and business owners. One of the best ways to learn and grow!"

—Julie Cole, Mabel's Labels

"**Moms Mean Business** is bridging the gap between what people perceive to be two different things: a career and a life. The two are actually in effect the same thing, especially when being done by women who tend to be at the helm of home lives in general. Calling someone a mompreneur is just a whole lot of labeling, which only serves to dilute the reality that we have a host of interests and responsibilities that comprise a life. This is the conversation we should be having—it's about being human, being a competent and confident woman."

—Kelsey Ramsden

"There are plenty of business books out there. And some of them cover some facets of being a woman entrepreneur. But getting the real scoop on mom entrepreneurship? This is it. Lara and Erin have done a brilliant job of pinpointing exactly what a mom entrepreneur needs to examine before, during, and after the launch of her company. I highly recommend it!"

— Jill Salzman, Founding Moms

"Finally! A book for mom entrepreneurs that doesn't tell us we can have it all! **Moms Mean Business** is refreshing in its approach as well as chock full of awesome tips and tools to help you get out of your own way, set realistic business goals, and work smarter so you can enjoy life and parenthood."

—Jyl Johnson Pattee, Mom It Forward

"When it comes to juggling home, family, and business, you need a trusted partner to help you figure things out and a custom plan that considers your unique family and your business goals. **Moms Mean Business** is like having someone in your corner saying, 'We're gonna make this work.'"

—Carley Knobloch, Carley K

The Top 10 Signs You Need to Read **Moms Mean Business**

1. **You work—a lot.** You're working longer hours and making less money than you want to. The lack of money causes you to work even harder in hopes of figuring out how to generate more income. It's a self-perpetuating cycle that you see no end to.

2. **Your kids can't tell time.** You want to be a good mom and you have visions of raising smart cookies, but your kids have learned from you that "Just a minute!" means the vast period of time between when they ask you for something and when you're actually able to stop working to answer them.

3. **You have no idea what we mean by "self-care."** Those friends of yours who get regular spa treatments? Well, you just can't relate to them at all. The closest you've come to self-care lately involves roaming the aisles at the grocery store while checking work e-mails on your phone.

4. **You think sleep is for the weak.** You learned when you had your first baby that sleep is something you can do without. Now that the kids sleep through the night, it's the perfect time to get caught up on your work. Sure, it takes a while for the computer key impressions to wear

off your face since you often fall asleep on the keyboard, but it's no big deal.

5. **You don't have time to plan your time.** Planning is great for people who don't have a lot going on. Your work keeps you so busy that things like business planning and marketing strategies are luxuries you certainly can't aspire to any time soon.

6. **You forgot your husband's name.** Yes, of course, you can remember it when you really try, without even having to look at his driver's license. But, mostly he's someone you really hope to re-connect with at some point, and until then, his name takes up too much mental space for you to recall on a regular basis, especially since you have to keep all those children's names straight.

7. **Your friends don't even try to get together with you anymore.** It's okay. Really. They will likely still be there for you when you come up for air. In the meantime, who needs the support and laughter that only girlfriends can provide?

8. **You can't figure out what to make for dinner.** After making 1,347 decisions today about everything from whether your daughter can sign up for hockey class after school, whether you should sign up for the flexible home heating program, to how you are going to source the materials for your product when your favorite vendor has gone out of business, you just don't have it in you to make one. More.

Decision. Dry cereal for dinner is nutritious. It says so right on the box.

9. **You can't remember why you thought this was such a good idea.** You put on a good face when those family members and neighbors ask you why you want to run your own business, but truthfully, you realize that your answers have just become a habit, like saying "Hello?" when the phone rings. You must have thought this business was a really good idea at some point. Right now, though, you've never been more exhausted in your life.

10. **You're ready.** You have a business or an idea for one and you're ready to move forward in a deliberate way to create the successful and happy life you deserve.

Let's get started.

Moms Mean Business

Moms Mean Business

A GUIDE TO CREATING
A SUCCESSFUL COMPANY AND
HAPPY LIFE AS A

Mom Entrepreneur

Erin Baebler *and*
Lara Galloway

CAREER
PRESS

Pompton Plains, N.J.

MOMS MEAN BUSINESS
EDITED AND TYPESET BY KARA KUMPEL
Cover design by Joanna Williams Design
Printed in the U.S.A.

To order this title, please call toll-free 1-800-CAREER-1 (NJ and Cana-da: 201-848-0310) to order using VISA or MasterCard, or for further information on books from Career Press.

**ᗃ CAREER
  PRESS**

The Career Press, Inc.
220 West Parkway, Unit 12
Pompton Plains, NJ 07444
www.careerpress.com

Library of Congress Cataloging-in-Publication Data
Galloway, Lara.
Moms mean business : a guide to creating a successful company and happy life as a mom entrepreneur / by Lara Galloway and Erin Baebler.
    pages cm
Includes bibliographical references and index.
ISBN 978-1-60163-350-7 -- ISBN (invalid) 978-1-60163-410-8 (ebook) 1. Businesswomen. 2. Home-based businesses. 3. Business planning. 4. Time management. I. Baebler, Erin. II. Title.

HD6053.G344 2014
658.1'10852--dc23
                                                              2014021300

To Matt, whose unwavering support made me believe that I could write and publish a book.

—Erin

For my first mom, Patti, whom I wish could've read this book.

—Lara

Acknowledgments

I am incredibly grateful to so many people who supported me and encouraged me throughout this process. It's been a very long road, and my friends and family never wavered in their belief that I could achieve my goal of writing this book and achieving my dream of becoming a published author. Special thanks to my husband, Matt; my children, Quin and Scarlett; my mom, Jan, and my step-dad, Mike; my dad, Brian, and my step-mom, Jenifer; my brother Steve and my sister-in-law Deni; my other brothers and sisters, Sean, Caitlin, Jenny, Brian, Melissa, and Ali; my mother-in-law, Mary; and my great friends, especially Traci, Kristi, Carolyn, Karleen, Barb, Jen, Andria, Gabby, Kathryn, Joanne, and Laura, who have all cheered me on over the years.

I am grateful to all of the moms who gave their time to share their experiences with us and with our readers. Each of you is an inspiration to me and our book is better than it would otherwise be thanks to your words of wisdom.

Moms Mean Business is an extension of the work I do, and I would be remiss if I didn't mention the special group of women who were in my coach certification class way back in 2006. We have all kept in touch and witnessed each other's trials and triumphs these past eight years, and I hope it will continue for many more. Thank you to Akasha, Barb, Constance, Erin, Katherine, Kathy, Kathy, Jane, and Martha.

Thank you to our agent, Jill Marsal, for believing in the book and in our ability to write it. Your input was invaluable. Thank you, also, to our two interns: Emily Ross, who worked with me several years ago before I even started the manuscript; and Shannon Duffy, who did some great research for us as we were finishing it up. Jacqueline Ernst at *www.ernstconnected.com* created our graphics, and we couldn't be more grateful. And, to Carley Knobloch, thanks for introducing me to Lara and unknowingly setting us up for this journey together.

Lastly, to my coauthor and now friend, Lara: Thank you for saying yes, thank you for making me laugh, thank you for your intelligence, determination, and groundedness, and most of all, thanks for being an amazing partner on this journey.

—Erin

It takes a village. I consider myself so lucky to be surrounded by the family and friends I have. First and foremost, I'm grateful to my biggest fans: my dad, Justin; my mom, Cecilia; and my little sister, Jessica, who believe that I can do whatever it is I try to do, even when I'm not sure I can. Your support and love mean everything to me. To my in-house team: thanks to my husband, Richard, for putting up with me when this book project took over my life; and to my littles, Charlie, Paul, and Ellie who give the best hugs and encouragement a mom could ever ask for.

I appreciate so much the powerful friends in my life who have helped shape my thoughts on what it means to be a mom, but also what it means to be me. Much love to Shelagh, Nicola, and Caragh for all the hours we have collectively spent together working out solutions to a woman's greatest challenges.

Thank you to all my clients, my social media buddies, and my podcast listeners for teaching me what it looks like to be a mom entrepreneur. This book is a collection of your stories and your lives, and I am truly in awe of all the good you do every day.

I'm so grateful to our agent, Jill Marsal, for seeing the value of our project and then helping us get it out into the world. You started the ball rolling for us. We'd like to give a huge shout-out to all the talented women who endorsed our book. It means so much to have your support. Thanks to Jacqueline Ernst for helping turn our words into graphics and for putting up with dozens of tiny tweaks to make them just right.

Finally, thanks to you, Erin, for having the vision for this book so long ago and for asking me to join you in it. I've had to pinch myself many times wondering how I got so lucky. Who knew writing a book together could be so much fun? This is just the beginning of a long friendship.

—Lara

Contents

Preface

*M*om entrepreneur. It's one of those phrases that has a lot of emotion behind it for some people. Why not *woman entrepreneur*? Or just *entrepreneur*? Some of our contributors bristled a bit when we mentioned the title and that we were writing specifically for *mom entrepreneurs*. For some, these words conjure up thoughts of not being taken seriously. Of not being thought of as a "real" entrepreneur. Or of being limited in some other way. As it turns out, using the word *mom* as a qualifier is a bit controversial.

For some of the women we spoke with, being labeled a *mom entrepreneur* comes with a huge responsibility. Because society still treats business owners who are also moms as a fairly new thing, or even as a novelty of sorts, some of these women feel as though it's up to them to pave the way. It's up to them to make sure that they succeed. To these women, it feels like a lot is riding on them having successful and happy lives with the path they've chosen. It reminds us of something Clare Booth Luce said: "Because I am a woman, I must make unusual efforts to succeed. If I fail, no one will say, 'She doesn't have what it takes.' They will say, 'Women don't have what it takes.'" Substitute the word *mom* for *woman*, and the stakes seem even higher.

For our purposes, *mom entrepreneur* means just that: a business owner who is a mom, or, if you prefer, a mom who is a business owner. What that looks like for each person is unique. For some, that may mean you only work while your children are at school or napping. For others, it may mean you run a large corporation and work long hours away from home. It doesn't matter what it looks like as long as what you do works for you. Sheryl Sandberg has gotten a lot of criticism for her book *Lean In*, but what she does beautifully throughout the book is point out that *leaning in* looks different for different women. We've got to stop comparing ourselves to others. We've got to stop feeling bad for the choices we've made. And we've got to stop judging each other for choices that don't involve us.

Moms Mean Business aims to help mom business-owners create a path for success in their careers and in their personal lives that fits with who they are and what they want for themselves and their families.

Introduction

What does it take to be a successful and happy mom entrepreneur? More importantly, what will it take for *you* to be a successful and happy mom entrepreneur? Because you've picked up this book, it's likely that you either dream of starting a business or you already own one. Maybe you have nagging doubts about your ability to be both a mom and a business owner with the time you have available. Maybe you're already doing both but feel as though you aren't doing either as well as you'd like to. Or maybe you have so many details coming at you on a daily basis that you aren't even sure where to put your focus.

We all have a different set of circumstances that make up our lives, and those circumstances are always shifting, so the experience of being both a mom and a business owner is different for each of us. There just isn't a one-size-fits-all plan. But, by being really clear about who you are and what you want, and by setting up systems that take some of the guesswork out of your every decision, chances are good that you can create your very own winning combination and be as successful as you want to be. With the help of this book, you will craft a powerful and sustainable plan that will get you on your way to the happiness and satisfaction you deserve.

One thing we've seen again and again is that the road to success for a mom entrepreneur is not always straight. In fact, more often than not it's quite crooked. It evolves with twists and turns along the way. Because of time constraints, conflicting priorities, and the constantly changing demands in our lives, our path just doesn't follow the linear steps laid out in many business books. We can also just about guarantee that your success (and your business) will have stops and starts—and possibly complete stalls. And, in addition to measuring things like year-over-year sales and profit margins, moms need permission to use criteria such as fulfillment and satisfaction to evaluate achievement both in business and in life.

Here's the thing about being a mom and a business owner: a different math applies. Often, we don't have a 40-hour work week with eight dedicated hours a day. And, as we mentioned before, it's usually not a linear path at all. It's a big leap forward followed by a standstill. It's long hours for two days followed by a day of not working much at all. It's figuring out child care while also arranging a business trip. Or it's trying not to feel guilty for truly enjoying what you do for a living. For many, it's finishing the workday once the kids are in bed.

The journey of a mom entrepreneur often looks and feels...hmmmm, what's a good word? *Creative? Crooked? Crappy? Exhilarating? Exciting? Exhausting?* Yes, it's all of those things. And because it doesn't necessarily follow an established series of steps along the way, you may be on the right path and not even realize it. You may be well on your way to creating all that you want and still think, *Well, this can't be right. It doesn't look like what I thought it would look like. And, it sure as heck isn't unfolding the way I thought it would.* Guess what? It probably doesn't and it most likely won't. Noticing those discrepancies is a sign that you need to let go of what you thought it would be like and embrace the way it is.

We aren't saying that you can just kick back, go with the flow, and see where it all takes you. Nope. We wholeheartedly believe in having a plan, and this book will help you with that. What we are saying, though, is that there is more than one way to get where you are going, and because your way will be based on the choices that are right for you, it will likely look different from what you think it should look like, and it will *definitely* look different from what you've seen in others' lives. The great part is, if you follow along with this book, it will look like *you* and it will uniquely and fabulously fit with your life.

Having coached hundreds of mom entrepreneurs, we've noticed that owning a business doesn't always lead to the happiness and sense of accomplishment that you might expect. Because mom entrepreneurs often dive in without fully considering their commitments and without making a comprehensive plan that addresses all the components of their lives, they can easily end up being pulled in several different directions. Let's face it: being a mom and owning a business can feel like a real conflict at times. And, because moms who start businesses are usually seeking flexibility and some semblance of balance, many potentially successful mom entrepreneurs end up disappointed because they find themselves either working the long hours they were trying to avoid in the first place or feeling as though they were being pulled in several different directions.

After all, being your own boss means you are in charge—of everything. And we're guessing that you bring the same high standards you learned and practiced while working for someone else into your own business. You want—and expect—the best in all areas of your life, so the pressure you put on yourself to excel can be intense. In fact, many mom entrepreneurs end up throwing in the towel before they've given their businesses a fair chance to get off the ground. Following our plan will allow you to keep moving toward your goals and will alleviate some of this pressure, making the whole journey feel a lot more manageable.

There will be challenges, of course, but women have some distinct strengths when it comes to running a business. We've all heard that a large portion of new businesses fail in the first year or two, but motherhood brings with it a useful perspective and set of skills that we believe can help increase your chances of success. According to a CBSNews report, women adapt better to new situations, make better managers and leaders, and invest more wisely than their male counterparts.[1] And according to a survey by Harvard Business Review, women are rated higher than men when it comes to building relationships.[2] In addition, motherhood fosters the ability to multitask, makes women experts at dealing with challenges as they come, and enhances both flexibility and problem-solving skills. Ultimately, living with multiple roles and conflicting priorities forces us to become effective and productive managers, which is one of the top skillsets we need as business owners.

The bottom line is that this journey is full of challenges, rife with possibilities, and, above all, unique for each and every mom entrepreneur. And, although that may seem like a grab bag of ambiguity, it's actually quite liberating once you embrace it because it means that you don't have to abide by the rules; your business doesn't have to follow a certain trajectory, and how it all goes down is pretty much up to you.

We know this uncertainty can be disconcerting at first. In fact, things may not look at all the way you think they should or how you want them to look. Even with the large number of women jumping into this realm, being both a mom and an entrepreneur still involves largely uncharted territory. There is no paved trail for creating a business when so many of our priorities contradict each other. Our business is *one* of the things that we put our focus on, but we have so many others: our kids, our house, our partner (if we have one), our need to exercise, and our obsession with certain reality TV shows. So, how are we supposed to determine success and how do we achieve that success when there is not one clear way to get there?

We wish there was one master recipe, that if you mixed a little bit of hard work with tenacity and wisdom, you'd end up wildly successful. For a lucky few, that simple combination probably works. For others, long hours and passion can lead to toiling away for years and still not reaching the level of accomplishment they hope for. There are many things you can do, though, to affect the outcome. In Chapter 6 specifically, we'll show you the different stages of business and what you can reasonably expect from each of them. In addition, from working with mom entrepreneurs throughout the years, we have homed in on some necessary foundational work that can be tremendously helpful for you and your well-being.

We've seen that establishing a solid foundation by being really clear about who you are, what your life is like, and what you want can launch you toward success more efficiently. We've observed that managing your time in an intentional way definitely adds to productivity and a sense of accomplishment. We've noticed that fully using the resources you have available as well as constantly adding to them is advantageous in many ways. And we know from our clients' experience and from our own that you'll need to be prepared to make adjustments along the way. We call it *truing yourself up*. *Moms Mean Business* presents the information you need to complete these essential steps, which means that, by reading and doing the exercises in this book, you'll be on your way to the success you both want and deserve.

How do we know? We've been there. Heck, we *are* there! We are certified life and business coaches and we are mom entrepreneurs. We've written a book together, but our paths to this point were very different. We don't claim to be sudden experts. We came by our knowledge honestly—by that we mean we've toiled and made mistakes, and fumbled, and persevered. We've both had moments that made us wonder if what we are doing is worth our time and effort. We've also had times when we've pinched ourselves to make sure this whole thing isn't all a glorious dream. Mostly, we've had days filled with choices, and priorities, hard work, hiccups, and contentment.

In addition to having our own experiences to draw from, we also coach other mom business-owners so we've seen how this quest looks for a lot of different women. The good news again: it looks different for everyone. The bad news again: it looks different for everyone. There is no easy-to-follow template for managing a successful life while you strive to also create a successful business. But, by capitalizing on your strengths, using all of your resources, creating a plan, mapping out your time, holding yourself accountable, and taking care of yourself along the way, we think your chances of success increase—greatly.

To show you what we mean, we've enlisted the help of some real-life mom entrepreneurs. Women, and perhaps moms in particular, are eager to hear how others manage it all. We are constantly looking for tips on how to move forward, how to handle everything that comes our way, how to create success on our own terms, and how to keep our sanity throughout the process. This is just as true when it comes to our businesses. When other women are willing to pull back the curtain to show us what life looks like from their perspective, it is beyond inspiring. In fact, the best lessons in life are often learned through trials and tribulations—our own and those of others. Stories of over-coming obstacles and learning from mistakes are powerful teachers, so we hope you'll benefit greatly from the words of wisdom provided by a group of mom entrepreneurs we admire.

Throughout *Moms Mean Business*, we'll peek into the lives of some of today's most successful mom business-owners, giving you a behind-the-scenes view of how they make their lives work—both personally and profession-ally. Watch for their stories in the "Moms Talk" sections you'll find included in each chapter. Luckily, moms who are farther down the path are usually more than willing to share their experience, especially if they know it will be helpful to someone else.

Is there a secret to these moms' success? Of course there is, and it's all in the approach they take from the start. Growing and managing a business that is designed to fit in with their already-full lives is the key to creating the fulfillment and satisfaction they had imagined. *Moms Mean Business* shows you how to do it too.

We hope the stories and words of wisdom will make the journey more recognizable and achievable for you. We hope you'll find inspiration and that all-important "me too!" factor. You may even find some remarkable similari-ties to your own situation. Just remember, your path is yours alone so it doesn't have to look like anyone else's. In fact, take this book as a permission slip: you are hereby given permission to have your trek toward being a success-ful mom entrepreneur reflect you and the life you lead. We'll say it again: it doesn't have to look a certain way and it may not closely resemble anyone else's journey—in fact, it probably won't. Just take the insight that you find useful and apply it to your life.

We know your time as a mom and a business owner is limited, which is why we have kept this book short, sweet, and accessible. Here's what you can expect:

Part I is the foundational first step: you have to know yourself, you have to acknowledge your priorities and values, you have to take stock of your circumstances, and you have to know how all of these inform you as you make decisions about your future. In Part I, we're going to hold up a mirror so you can see where you are today and get clear about where you want to go. We'll start with a quick but informative assessment so you can see how you're doing, then lead you through some exercises so you can articulate all of the things that are important to you. Then we'll have you envision what you want for the future, creating your own definition of success in the process. Because it's the number-one issue moms deal with, you will also take a close look at your time: how you spend it, how you can use it more effectively, and how you can protect it.

Because *you* are the most important component of all this, we'll show you how to build in the time and a plan for self-care. This will allow you to make huge strides forward while acknowledging the importance of your well-being. Owning a business while being a mom has the potential for burnout, so you'll need to build in some time to relax, play, exercise, and just be. So many women put themselves at the bottom of their to-do lists, which is such a huge mistake. If you want to have a thriving business while raising a thriving family, you'll need to build in some time for yourself to thrive as well. We'll help you decide what that looks like for you so that it becomes automatic and guilt-free. All of this groundwork will create a solid foundation from which to launch or grow your business. This initial work is a crucial and often overlooked first step for mom entrepreneurs looking for success and satisfaction.

Part II is about getting your business from Point A to Point B, and managing it all. You will take stock of your strengths, skills, past experiences, and other valuable resources so you can leverage them as you start or grow as an entrepreneur. You will also determine what stage your business is in, create a business plan, and determine how best to move forward in a way that meshes with who you are and what you envision as well as with the time you have available. We'll address productivity and introduce specific time-management techniques and tools that will help you accomplish more in less time. You will also create a personalized system of accountability that will enable you to do the things you want to do. Accountability is a straightforward and easy-to-use tool that will help you stay on track. Don't be fooled by its simplicity, though. It is a powerful little puppy. We'll also talk about how to handle the dips, delays, roadblocks, and other frustrations that you are sure to meet along the way so that when you do, you can learn from them, recover quickly, and keep moving forward. By the end of Part II, you will know what you need to do, when you need to do it, and how you'll get it done.

Whether you're just starting out or growing an existing business, we know it takes a lot to succeed as both a mom and a business owner. Along the way, we'll root for you from the pages. Consider us your personal professional coaches and also your cheerleaders (though not the kind who wear those short skirts and have glitter in their hair). *Moms Mean Business* is a powerful, portable reference book that helps you create a successful and happy life as a mom entrepreneur. The point is, we know you can do it, and we're here to offer you as much support along the way as we possibly can. Enjoy the stories and interviews from the women who have gone before you. Enjoy the process of figuring out what will work best for you. And enjoy the time and effort that goes into creating something that supports you, fulfills you, and lets you know just what you can do when you put your mind to it. You've got this. We just know it!

Part I

Own Your Life

Chapter 1

Who You Are

So you think you want to start a business. Or maybe you already have but it's not yet as swimmingly successful as you'd hoped. Or maybe it's successful but you don't feel the sense of satisfaction you had expected. Whatever the situation, it's important to be clear about who you are and what you are setting out to do. As you know, things don't always go the way you imagined they would. That's why having both a strong foundation and a solid plan is so important. They will help you weather the storms and endure the inevitable setbacks.

There are serial entrepreneurs out there who simply look for viable businesses and a market that will buy their wares so they can make some money. But in all our years of coaching mom entrepreneurs, not one of our clients has chosen this approach to business. Instead, most moms tend to yearn for purposeful work that provides us the freedom, flexibility, and fulfillment we crave. We want to be there for our child(ren), and we want to do work that matters to us. Of course, we also want to make money, but if that's the only thing driving you, there are easier ways to make a living than owning a business.

We'll begin with a surprise. (Who doesn't love a good surprise?) The first step toward planning your business as a mom entrepreneur actually has nothing to do with the business at all. Nope, this first big step is not determining what the business is, but *who you are*. It doesn't matter at this point what you plan on selling or how you plan to market and deliver it. (Of course, these elements *are* critical, but we'll sort them out later.) What matters is who you are and what your unique goals are.

Designing your own path might not be as simple as you think it is, because it's easy to be swayed by outside forces. In fact, you might be living a life that turned out the way it did because it's what your mom wanted for you. It could be the way it is because it's what your partner thought was best. Or it could be that you created your current life based on what seemed safest or what felt like the path of least resistance. We are bombarded with messages from the media, from friends and family, and even from our own inner voice about how things are "supposed" to be. So as you go through the exercises in this book, we challenge you to check in to make sure the voice that is answering the questions is your own. It's absolutely essential to answer the questions for yourself without worrying about what others expect from you or what you think you *should* choose. From a space of calm reflection, we're going to ask you to purposefully reflect on how you want things to be. That's the only way to see what changes you need to make to *true up* your current life with the one you want going forward. It helps you quiet the noise that can so easily influence everything you do.

This is also a great time to look at the ideals and standards you might be trying to live up to. For instance, if you want your home to look like a Pottery Barn store or think your family should resemble the models in a J. Crew catalog, you have to be willing to do the work it takes to create a life like that. In other words, does spending a lot of your time and money on perfect hair and beautiful bookshelves correlate with the idea you have for your life and your business? If so, great! (We'd love to be invited over to hang out in that flawless house of yours.) If not, though, it's time to stop trying to achieve someone else's ideas of what life should look like. If you tend to judge yourself against some perfect version of what life can be, it's worth considering whether that version of life is really what you want. Even if everyone around you seems to want their life to look a certain way, that does not mean you have to want that too. We are talking about *your* life, after all, and as long as you spend your time and energy on what's most important to you, you're sure to be on a path that leads to your vision.

So let's find out more about you. Read the following statements and respond by placing a number from 1 to 10 in the blank. A 1 means you don't agree with the statement at all, and a 10 means that you agree with it completely. Choose the number that you feel best represents where you are right now.

_____ 1. My day-to-day life is filled with purposeful activities that align with my priorities and values.

_____ 2. I have my own definition of success and a plan to achieve it.

_____ 3. I have a good balance of work time, family time, and personal time in my typical week.

_____ 4. My work is fulfilling and I look forward to it most days.

_____ 5. My day-to-day activities utilize and highlight my strengths, skills, and style in a way that makes me feel as though I contribute to my family and community.

_____ 6. I'm clear on my priorities and make sure that they show up first and foremost in my life.

_____ 7. I almost always choose activities that play to my strengths and try to limit tasks that don't.

_____ 8. My family and friends support my choices, encourage me to be my best self, and help me when I need it.

_____ 9. I spend time planning for the future, have an idea of what is next for me, and know when it will all likely happen.

_____ 10. I'm energized by my work and excited about the future.

_____ 11. My time is well spent and I am usually able to avoid being late and feeling rushed.

_____ 12. I say no to opportunities that I simply don't have time to take on.

_____ 13. I build and maintain strong connections with people who can help me and with those whom I can help.

_____ 14. I have a strong sense of who I am and what's most important to me.

_____ 15. I am living a life that works for me, not the life that someone else expected me to live.

_____ 16. I have good stress relief habits and take extra care with myself when I start to feel tension creeping in.

_____ 17. I make sure I have free time to do the things I love to do.

_____ 18. I know I can't do it all on my own and I regularly ask for help when I need it.

_____ 19. My work has a meaningful purpose for me.

_____ 20. I find time to fit in fun with family and friends on a regular basis.

_____ 21. I take good care of myself physically by eating well and finding time to work out.

_____ 22. I feel as though I can keep up with my life, and I know how to keep from getting overwhelmed by all of the little things coming at me on a daily basis.

_____ 23. I take ample time away from work, including days off during the week and weeks off during the year.

_____ 24. I have realistic expectations about what I can get done during this phase of my life.

_____ 25. I feel as though I have enough time to work steadily toward my goals and aspirations.

This assessment is meant to provide you with a snapshot of your life in this moment. Follow these scoring directions to better understand which areas need your attention:

Total the scores you gave for questions 1, 4, 6, 14, and 24. This score will help you understand how well you know and honor the things that are most important to you.

Write the total here: _____

If your score is between 40 and 50, you likely have a strong sense of your values, motivations, and priorities, and you do a good job of making sure that your life reflects those things.

A mid-range score (25–39) may indicate that you either aren't clear on what makes you tick, or, even if you are clear, your day-to-day life doesn't reflect that very well.

A score of 24 or lower probably means that you need to make this area a priority for now. Pay special attention to the parts of your life that aren't going the way you'd

like them to and spend some time getting clear about your
needs and wants.

Now total the scores you gave for questions 2, 9, 10,
15, and 19.

Write the total here: _____

If your score is between 40 and 50, you likely have a
very strong understanding of what you want for your future. Being able to clearly envision success on your own
terms makes you well equipped to pursue and reach your
goals.

A mid-range score (25–39) indicates that you have
some ideas about what you want but that those ideas could
be even more focused. Scoring in the middle range here
might also mean that you need to make sure that your
definition of success is yours and yours alone.

A score of 24 or lower indicates that you would benefit from spending some time thinking about all that you
want in both your life and your business. Once you do,
you'll feel more in charge and begin to notice big changes
in your life.

Now total the scores you gave for questions 3, 11,
12, 22, and 25. These questions have to do with time
management.

Write the total here: _____

A high score here (40–50) shows that you have a great handle on how you spend your time and how you schedule your days.

A score in the middle range (25–39) reveals that you could make some simple changes when it comes to your schedule that will allow you to get more done in less time.

A score lower than 25 means that you likely spend your days rushing around without much to show for the time spent. Pay special attention to managing your time and implement some small changes that will make your days less harried and more productive. (We'll show you how to do that later.)

Now total the scores you gave for questions 16, 17, 20, 21, and 23. These questions have to do with self-care.

Write the total here: _____

A high score here (40–50) shows that you most likely have a good self-care routine in place. Keep up the good work and look for ways to add to it.

A score of 25 to 39 lets you know that there is some work to be done here. As moms, we tend to forget to put ourselves on our to-do list. As a mom entrepreneur, you simply can't afford to make that mistake. Make it a priority to create some self-care habits.

A low score (less than 24) means you have a lot of room for improvement. Focusing on this area and adding in some specific self-care routines will set you on your way to making yourself a priority and ensuring that you'll have the stamina to handle all that comes your way.

Now total the scores you gave for questions 5, 7, 8, 13, and 18.

Write the total here: _____

If you are conscious of your strengths, skills, and talents, and use them to your benefit on a regular basis, it's likely **you scored a 40 or higher.**

A score between 25 and 39 indicates that you need to become even more aware of all that you have available to you and how you can use those things to benefit you in both business and in life.

A score lower than 24 shows that you likely haven't taken the time to catalog all of your strengths, skills, and talents, and/or that you aren't leveraging them in a way that will help you get ahead.

Use this assessment to better understand the areas of your life where you have things handled and where you need to do a bit of work. Small changes can have a big impact, so don't let a score that is lower than you'd like discourage you. This assessment is just a starting point. Because the goal of this book is to help you increase your satisfaction with your life and your work, let's keep going.

Your Values, Motivators, Priorities, and Passions

First we're going to spend some time looking at your values, your motivators, your priorities, and your passions. For many of us, these things can be interchangeable, and when you're making a list of each of them, you will likely find some overlap. For instance, if you value family, you might also be very motivated by taking good care of your family, and family might also show up as both a priority and a passion. That's okay. In fact, that can even make it easier for you because when something makes it on more than one of your lists, you are pretty likely to pay attention to it. When we are talking about values, motivators, priorities, and passions, we are talking about the things that are most important to who you are and how you operate. When you have a good understanding of what those things are, you are going to have a much easier time making the decisions, changes, and choices you need to make in your life and in your business.

You are going to articulate some of the things that are most important to you and some of the things that will help drive you forward. You'll likely notice that it's not possible to give equal attention to each of them every day. For example, if innovation and independence are two of your top values or motivators but you find yourself in a financial hole, you may need to leave those on the shelf for a while so you can earn the money you need to keep your family afloat. That doesn't mean you are abandoning those things altogether; sometimes you just have to take care of the basics first. Once you are stable again, that's the time to start looking at how you can honor your need for innovation and independence. When you know what your values, motivators, priorities, and passions are, you can almost effortlessly create some effective guideposts for future happiness and satisfaction.

Now grab a pen and some paper. Throughout this book, when you see this icon

you'll know you need to be ready to make some notes or answer some questions.

Your Values

Imagine that you're 90 years old. You look back on your life, and you feel incredibly satisfied with what you see. At this ripe old age, you've gotten rid of the *should*s in your life and you spend your days doing the things that matter most to you. You no longer worry about every little hiccup or what other people think. You're at peace.

From this place of wisdom, think about what is most important to you. In coach-speak, we call these things values. As the name suggests, these are the things on which we place the most value in both life and work, and they are also some of the things by which we (consciously or subconsciously) measure ourselves to see if our life is turning out the way we had hoped it would. Our values are often integral traits that remain fairly consistent throughout our lives, so checking in with them is a great way to figure out why we don't feel as satisfied as we want to.

When we live in a way that matches our core values, we feel satisfied and the road feels smooth. Conversely, when our values are out of whack, the opposite is true. So you can see how important it is to make a conscious effort to identify and live by your own values. Although largely inherent, your personal values can evolve in time, because *you* evolve in time, so it's important to revisit them. Failing to consciously identify and keep track of your values can lead to a lot of frustration and wasted effort. Because we want the opposite of frustration and wasted effort for you, we suggest you take a moment to think about and journal on your top five values right now.

Here is a brief list to get you going. This list is far from exhaustive so feel free to come up with your own words that express your personal values.

abundance	achievement	adventure
creativity	excellence	family
freedom	friendship	health

honesty	humor	independence
inner harmony	integrity	joy
kindness	loyalty	order
personal development	power	recognition
relationships	responsibility	respect
security	simplicity	trust
wealth	wholeness	wisdom

Now that you know what we mean by values and have had a chance to think about it, write down your top five values.

Your Motivations

What motivates you in life and in business? What keeps you going day after day? You need to know the answer to these questions whether you're just starting to think about creating a business or you are already running one. Is this work something you feel you were meant to do? Is it the kind of work that makes you thrilled to get up in the morning? Is it work that came about because you saw a problem in the world that you knew you could fix? Does it help provide the life you want for your family? Whatever your motivation is, you need to name it and own it. Your motivators will always be there, helping you make choices and moving you toward your goals, so make sure you are clear on what is driving you.

We've worked with women who thought they were working for one reason, but after giving it careful thought, realized they were actually motivated to run their own companies because of some very strong beliefs, goals, or dreams. For example, one of our clients started a company simply believing she had a marketable idea for a product. One thing led to another, and the fairly quick success of her brand proved that she had been right. However, she soon realized that in order to really feel successful, she needed to acknowledge and act on her strong desire to give back to her community. It wasn't something that was in her business plan from the beginning but it became a driving force for her company.

Being clear about what motivates you will be especially important when you hit a rough patch. On those days, getting in touch with your motivators will help you keep going even if you feel like giving up.

Spend a few minutes thinking about what motivates you. Here are some common motivators:

- Flexibility
- Autonomy
- Freedom
- Your children
- Building a better life
- Helping others
- The desire to create something
- Ability to give back
- Doing something you love

We could go on and on, but now it's your turn. Ask yourself about your main motivations and write them down.

Your Priorities

Our goal is for you to get to a place where you can keep up with all of the responsibilities and tasks in your personal life *and* manage your business. The best way to do this is to get really clear on the things that matter the most to you: your priorities. This is one of the biggest factors that sets mom entrepreneurs apart from other entrepreneurs. Although everyone gets to decide for him- or herself what his or her priorities are, when you are a mom, your priorities always include your kids in one way or another. Priorities have a huge function in the life of a mom entrepreneur. They become your boss. By that we mean that it's your priorities that will help you decide where to put your focus and how best to spend your time.

Your most valuable asset—and also your scarcest re-source—is your time. Your kids need you, your clients need you, your partner needs you, your team needs you... and that's just the beginning. The school fundraising com-mittee wants your help with the auction. Your mother is hoping you will plan this year's family reunion. You'd re-ally like to spend some quality time volunteering the way you used to. Perhaps, if you try really hard and are a mas-ter multitasker you can get all that done and still make time to be the snack mom for your son's soccer game or your daughter's swim meet.

How on earth can a mom entrepreneur do it all? The obvious answer is, she can't. You can't. If you want to run a business while raising a family, you're going to need to get comfortable saying the word *no* a lot more than you're used to. There is no way anyone can do it all, and, hon-estly, we don't see the value of trying. Even though you can't do it all, you can do the things you really want to do. And that's a consideration we're going to ask you to make: saying no to some things means you'll be able to say yes to the things that matter the most. We'll go into this more in Chapter 3.

Moms Talk

I do have guilt. I have tons of it, and it's "moth-er guilt," it's "CEO guilt," it's "daughter guilt." You name it, I've got it. And I think it's because we feel like we have to be perfect in all we do. There is no way that you can do the perfect job at any of those if you're doing so many of them. So I think you have to trust that you're getting the big stuff done. What are the big priorities for you as a mother? Or what are the big priorities for you as a CEO? And focus on those. You have to let some stuff go.

—Sharelle Klaus, Dry Soda

I am pretty sure every working mama has guilt leaving her kids. In addition, I envisioned that I would be this picturesque wife, mom, friend, daughter, sister, and I am FAR from that. There are not enough hours in a day to be all of those things. I have a 7-month-old and a 3.5-year-old, and at this point in my life, I am just trying to survive! Truthfully, I don't deal with the guilt. It's always there, and it's always going to be there. I am working on accepting this fact, and doing the best that I can with the time that I have.

—Kristy Lewis, Quinn Popcorn

As a single mom running a very demanding business, my biggest hurdle every day is that I feel like there is never enough time. Looking at a daily to-do list can be very overwhelming and paralyzing because there's always so much to do. I find that asking myself, "What's on my A-list today?" helps tremendously to prioritize and get perspective on what's most important. Taking care of the must-dos first helps clear my mind so I can focus on what's next.

—Debra Gano, BYOU (Be Your Own You) Magazine

For now, we want you to pick the four main priorities in your life. That's right—only four. You see, for it to be called a *priority*, you just can't have 17 things that are "most important." Some things matter more than others, and it's up to you to choose which ones are which. As we mentioned earlier, it's a really bad idea to ask others (your husband, your mother, or your friend) to decide on your priorities. It's also not a good idea to choose the things you think *should* be priorities. It takes courage to pick what matters most to you and to agree to let some of the other areas of your life be less important.

So what are your priorities? Here are some examples to get you started:

- Financial security
- Quality family time
- A healthy marriage
- A thriving business
- Saving for the future
- Children's education
- Physical health
- Personal wellbeing
- Being known as an expert
- Thriving children

Your priorities may come straight from this list or they may be completely different. That's the point. They are yours and yours alone. So, think about your life and the things that are truly the most important to you. These are the things that must be nurtured and paid attention to, no matter what.

Write down your top four priorities.

> *Things which matter most must never be at the mercy of things which matter least.*
> —Johann Wolfgang von Goethe

We like to say that integrity means keeping the promises you make to yourself. By choosing your priorities, you are promising that those are the things you'll take care of; those are the things that will get top billing in your life. If you say that health and well-being are priorities and then you take up smoking, well, that's a problem. When you fail to keep your promises to yourself, you create pain and angst that just don't need to be there. And, because we aren't able to compartmentalize things (as much as we'd like to think we can), guess what else is affected? Everything. Including your business.

> *In a country where the workplace is structured around an ideal worker who's on call 24/7 and motherhood is characterized by the model of a mother always available to her children, it's hard to balance work and family.*

—Joan C. Williams and Rachel Dempsey, *What Works for Women at Work: Four Patterns Working Women Need to Know*

That's why it is so important to be really honest when you are deciding on your priorities. We said this earlier, but it bears repeating: If you choose your priorities based on what you think should be important or based on what you think others might want you to say, you are setting yourself up for failure—both personally and professionally.

There's no way to be a perfect mother, and a million ways to be a good one.
—Jill Churchill

Once you have your priorities in place, it becomes much easier to decide if an activity or new opportunity is right for you. Let's say you've decided that growing your business is a top priority and that gaining exposure for your company is a smart way to work toward the growth you are looking for. Then suppose a colleague calls to ask you if you'd like to write a monthly blog post for her readers who fit your target market. Thanks to your list of priorities, you decide that it makes sense to simply add this task to your calendar or possibly stop doing something else to make time for this monthly activity. Voila! Suddenly your schedule closely matches up with your goals and priorities. In case you need us to connect the dots for you, that's a very good thing. We will talk about this more in Chapter 3.

We want to mention that priorities are not set in stone. They will change as you, your business, and your family grow and change. Because of that, we recommend taking a look at your priorities at least twice a year so you can make sure they are still a reflection of you, your life, and your goals. If they aren't, it's easy enough to make some adjustments.

Moms Talk

In 2010, I got my first $10 million project to widen the Alaska Highway. That spring my husband, Andrew, and I bought a house in London, Ontario. We both started our new jobs (his in London, mine in Fort St. John). Andrew moved into our new house on his own. Our daughter, Sophie, who was 2 at the time, was still with me, so we flew to London, I dropped her off with Andrew, and I left to run this big job for seven months by myself.

While I was away working on the job, Andrew and Sophie came to visit me for about six days. There was a lot of judgment around us—people were speculating that our marriage must be falling apart, that our arrangements were going to damage Sophie, and they were especially questioning how we could prioritize my business over our family.

But the reality is that our marriage grew stronger, our family grew stronger, the people in the business trusted us more, and Sophie will to this day say, "I love my dad because he took care of me when I was a baby." Dad had an opportunity to be the shining star in a marriage that works. I could have said, "No, I'm not taking this job," but it was a pivot point that positioned me to be where I am in my career and where we are in our life.

I truly lived out the notion that I believed I was capable of doing this thing very much on my own but also as a benefit to my family. Furthermore, I've always kept in the back of my mind the fact that Andrew's family has a history of heart attacks and strokes. I've always worried what would happen if he died at 50 and I end up on my own. I've had the opportunity to prove to myself that I really can handle all this. To hell with everyone's opinion of my marriage and my choices.

Of course, it goes both ways. There are times when I've said no to the bank, that I'm not coming in for a meeting because my daughter is sick, and in that moment, my family just trumped my business. I make no apologies to anyone.

—Kelsey Ramsden, Canada's Top Female Entrepreneur, Belvedere Place Development

Maybe when I'm at a different point in my life, when my kids get older or when I have more time to travel, I might get that loan, launch more products, and do all of the trade shows that I was so excited about. But now is not the time for that for me.

—Andreea Ayers, Launch Grow Joy

To me, managing priorities is about keeping focused on the big picture. There are many things that bring you joy in the world; your job is only one of them. I try to live a balanced life, and don't feel bad about treating myself right, because if I am healthy and happy I will be a better mother, wife, and business owner.

—Veronica Bosgraaf, PURE Bar

Your Passions

Let's not forget the power of your passions. *Passion* is one of those words that is volleyed to and fro, but what does it really mean? And how important is it when you're starting or growing a business? Passions are the things in life that excite you, the things that make you come alive. From talking to hundreds of mom entrepreneurs, we've come to realize that passion really can play a huge role in your quest for success. We've all heard the saying, attributed to Marsha Sinetar, that goes, "Do what you love and the money will follow." It doesn't always hold true, but we will say that success, financial and otherwise, does frequently follow when you are driven by a passion. We haven't encountered many mom entrepreneurs who are doing what they do just for the money. So, as you pursue your vision for your business, it's likely going to help if there is some aspect about it you love.

This doesn't mean you have to sell a product or provide a service that you are absolutely passionate about, though that is a big plus, of course. If you're not particularly passionate about your product, you should have a passion for at least a part of what you do. For instance, if you absolutely love to speak or write or create videos, make sure that you incorporate that passion into the way you promote your business. We'll give you an example: Lara loves sharing her experience by speaking to groups of people. Because of this, she makes sure that she pursues paid speaking gigs as part of her work with her company, Mom Biz Coach. Sure, there are still some parts of running her business that she is less passionate about, so she delegates and outsources as much of that as possible, knowing that it's always easier and more productive to do the things you love to do. If you can incorporate a passion into your business, it's like icing on the cake.

Moms Talk

Life is too short. If you have the passion to do something, go for it! Surround yourself with people who share in your vision and your passion. Work hard, accept failure, learn from it, and

move on. And don't forget to enjoy your successes and achievements.

—Grace Welch, Patemm Inc.

My business is derived completely from passion. I didn't choose it. The business chose me.
I saw a problem, which I knew I could fix, then
couldn't not fix it. The business ultimately formed
itself around those passion-driven actions over
the course of several years. What we do now, for
whom we do it, the people involved, the products we create, even our investors—there is no
part of our brand that isn't passion-driven. In the
early days, I spent many hours, which turned into
months, getting clear on our core values and deciding whether or not to launch into running a
business full-time—on whether or not to support
the business fully and let it grow. I didn't necessarily know the steps to get there, but once I made
the choice to start, there was really nothing that
could stop me.

Even still, 10 years later, I wake up every day
(at 3 or 4 a.m.) knowing that I could fail, but I don't
care. Today, staying true to our passions is at the
foundation of our core values and every decision
we make. The clarity our team has regarding the
value of our work keeps us going—we keep each
other going. And importantly, we all know where

we are going at the end of the day—at least at the high level. Ultimately those values are what allow us to make the toughest decisions and then trust in those decisions. If you are clear on who you are and what drives you, there is no decision too tough or too complex. Executing on any given decision could be ridiculously hard, but you never wonder what to do, just how to get it done. You know. And then simply have to be willing to connect the dots and accept any consequence.

—Kim Walls, Episencial

I started my business as a single mom of a 1-year-old with very little support. So often I wondered if I was crazy to be taking the risk. But my passion to help young girls was more powerful than my fear. Find what you are passionate about and that passion will draw support to you and outshine all the challenges that you encounter along the way.

—Debra Gano, BYOU (Be Your Own You) Magazine

In fact, if you never get the chance to pursue the things you are passionate about, you might wind up feeling dissatisfied. So, even if your business and your passions don't coincide, it's worth it to articulate what those passions are so you can look for ways to incorporate them into your life in another way. A potential hiccup is that some of us have either forgotten how to pursue them or have been told that pursuing them is only for the naïve. Some of us aren't even sure what they are anymore because we've been taught that going after them just isn't practical. Quiet those thoughts and think about the things you are passionate about.

As we mentioned, your passions make you come alive, and we can't think of a better way to pursue being both a mom and an entrepreneur than from a place of feeling absolutely full of life. With that in mind, think about what you are passionate about. Write down what comes to mind.

Follow your passion, and success will follow you.
—Terri Guillemets

Keep this list handy because passionate people are magnetic people. In addition, doing something you are passionate about can help you get back in touch with your-self when you hit the inevitable dips that happen when you own your own business—especially when you own a busi-ness and have the added responsibility of being a mom.

Your Life

It's such a broad heading: your life. What we mean by life in this context is all of the components and circum-stances that are part of your day-to-day existence. Those details give you clues about your values, attitudes, and desires. They can also help you uncover both your possibilities and your current limitations.

Moms Talk

Our path has had a very zigzag pattern to it, with many fits and starts. A few years back we decided we wanted to work together, so we brainstormed on how best to use our creative talents and professional strengths in a business venture. We both felt a readiness to work, but knew that the business had to enhance our individual lives while not detracting from our family lives. It was a practical approach, but also one that allowed us to stretch the possibilities of what our business could be without trying to squeeze ourselves into Cinderella's glass slipper.

Just as we formulated our business plans and were ready to launch, life got in the way. We found ourselves wooed by opportunities that led us back to our old careers. Fast-forward a few years and the commitment to get the business off the ground and the desire to work together were stronger than ever. We reached the point where we had to decide either to move forward or to put the idea to rest once and for all. We chose to keep going, and as soon as we did, everything started falling into place. Clients started calling and we found the perfect person to join our team. Making the commitment to the business—once we were both in the right place—started the ball rolling, and Tweak has continued to grow since then.

—Kathryn Cree Bouchard and Gabby Roffey, Tweak

Let's take a mental snapshot of your life as it is right now. Are you married? Separated? Divorced? Are you employed? Are you the main breadwinner for your family? Do you live in a city? In the suburbs? On a farm? How is your health? How is the health of your kids and/or partner? Do you need to exercise on a regular basis to feel your best or to manage a health condition? How old are your kids? How involved do you want or need to be in their activities? Is it important to you to be around when your kids get home from school? Do you cherish time alone or time with friends, or both? The circumstances of our lives are specific to us and have a profound impact on everything, so that's why we ask. Take a minute to acknowledge the details of your life. If you have young children who aren't yet in school, and you have a priority of spending a lot of time with them, then your business (and the rate at which it grows) will be different than it would be for someone whose children are at school or in the care of someone else during the workday. We aren't saying one is better than another. We are simply saying: take a close look at what is possible right now based on your circumstances *and* what's important to you. (If you need a reminder about what's most important to you, refer to the Priorities section.)

By the way, this is not meant to limit you. In fact, knowing your parameters will help you make realistic choices about how your business can move forward, which is actually very freeing. And, so that we aren't glossing this over, we also want you to be really honest with yourself when looking at your life circumstances. If, for instance, you are the sole breadwinner or you're pregnant or you're dealing with a health issue (either yours or someone else's), it may not be the right time to start or grow a business. That can be a hard truth to face, but it's better to face it than to struggle against the reality of your life. We could go on and on, but we bet you get the picture. The point we are making is that when you are a mom, the circumstances of your life are very important when it comes to choosing the work that you do. In fact, we might even go so far as to say that your circumstances (along with what's most important to you) dictate the work that is possible for you to do. With this in mind, write down the details of your life that could impact your ability to start or grow a business.

Assuming there are no deal-breakers in your list, let's move on to Chapter 2, where you will get a chance to envision your life in the future.

Bottom Line

✎ In order to begin creating a successful company and a happy life as a mom entrepreneur, you need to get clear on where you are today and what factors will impact you and your ability to start or grow a business.

✎ The four key elements that determine how we usually make decisions are our values, motivators, priorities, and passions.

✎ Be careful when you name your values, motivators, priorities, and passions. It's easy to feel influenced by what others want or what you think you *should* want.

✎ Take a close look at the circumstances of your life so you will know what's possible as well as any potential limitations that could affect your ability to own a business.

Chapter 2

Envisioning Success

Quick: When we say *success*, what comes to mind? Don't overthink it. Just say the word to yourself and jot down any thoughts that show up.

Now take a look at what you've written. What did you come up with? When thinking of success, did your first thoughts have to do with yourself, your family, and your business? Or did you imagine other people and their success? Sometimes when we ask our clients to do this simple exercise, they realize they don't even have a clear vision of themselves as successful. After all, when you're in the thick of raising kids, running a household, and creating or growing a business, when do you have time to ponder what success on your own terms looks like? And to be honest, sometimes the thought of big-time success is actually quite scary. Success inevitably means change—big change—and change interrupts the routines, the norms, and the familiar in our lives. On top of that, being wildly successful as a mom entrepreneur conjures up hard questions such as, *How will success affect my marriage? Can I stand the pressure of being the breadwinner in my family? Will I have as much time to hang out with my kids as I'm used to? What will people think of me and my priorities if I put the business first?* Fear of success is just as pervasive among women business owners as is fear of failure. If you fear success, well, you can imagine that it's going to be a challenge for you to achieve it.

It's also fairly easy to get caught up in living life in the fast lane without taking the time to think about how you are measuring your progress and accomplishments. And yet, whether you realize it or not, you are probably assessing yourself in some way or another: Perhaps you're thinking about the financial success (or lack thereof) of your business. Or you are gauging your success on the car you drive or the house you live in. You're not alone if those are the types of metrics you've unknowingly chosen. These are society's metrics, and it's pretty easy to fall in line and use these outward signs of success to determine whether you're on track or not. We happen to think that there's much more to success for a mom entrepreneur than the financial and/or outward successes that are easy enough to see. These simply don't tell the whole story.

Probably the most common way we measure ourselves without really thinking about it is by comparing ourselves to others. We read about people in magazines and on Facebook, or we watch them heading down the red carpet on TV, or we try to keep up with the neighbors down the street who appear to have the perfect house, the perfect lawn, and the perfect lives, or we envy those entrepreneurial superstars we always hear being interviewed on the radio for their latest amazing business that made them a million dollars. But comparing yourself to another mom entrepreneur, or another parent, or another business owner is not the same as defining success for yourself. In fact, it can be the complete opposite. Have you heard the saying, "To compare is to despair"? That seems to be just how it works out. When you compare yourself to someone else, you usually wind up feeling less than great about your life. Comparing yourself to others ensures that you will never measure up; there will always be someone who seems to be doing better than you are. And the feelings that crop up when you size up your life as compared to someone else's? You can bet those feelings and thoughts will hinder you rather than empower you to live the life you want to live. When you rely on comparisons, you are not trusting yourself to know what is best for you. Everyone has different backgrounds, different strengths, and different motivators, so trying to compare yourself to someone else really is pointless.

Another way we measure ourselves without even realizing it is by defining success too narrowly. If you've always thought that success would look a certain way—living in a certain neighborhood, driving a specific type of car, or vacationing twice a year in Tahiti—or if you have another aspiration that is very specific, you may have unwittingly set yourself up to feel like a failure no matter what you do. After all, until you reach that particular milestone, you've automatically fallen short. And, funny enough, even if you do reach it, you just might find yourself feeling disappointed. Setting your sights on one specific accomplishment can be very motivating, but basing your whole idea of success on that one achievement leaves out all of the different facets that go into creating a satisfying life beyond that accomplishment.

Maybe you have thought through this whole idea of being successful and know what it will look like for you. Let's say you've done some personal reflection and even some professional goal-setting, and you are clear on how you want your best life to look. That's awesome. But how long ago did you set those goals and create that vision? Is it possible that your definition of success is somewhat outdated, or even that it has since completely changed? Does it fit into the lifestyle you're living now? A vision board you created even two years ago could be way off the mark for you today—just ask someone who discovered she was unexpectedly pregnant, or someone who is now the sole breadwinner for her family since her partner was laid off last week, or the woman whose business took off and grew exponentially in ways she never planned. When it comes to helping you get what you want, an outdated vision of success is no more helpful than not having one at all.

Moms Talk

When I started my soap business, here's what I had imagined my business would look like in a few years: I would buy a piece of land, buy a yurt and some goats to get milk and make goat milk soap, hire local soap makers to make the soaps, work out of the yurt every day, and set up a shop on pedestrian-friendly Pearl Street in Boulder, Colorado, where I live. I would attend major tradeshows like NY Now, Atlanta Gift Market, International Home & Housewares Show, ACRE Las Vegas, San Francisco International Gift Show, ISPA Show, and a few others. It would give me a chance to travel, meet people face to face, and grow my brand. This sounded so exciting! But I realized this opportunity to expand the business would have required me to accelerate my business plans immediately—either take out loans to buy the land and move to the yurt, or buy space to open a soap-making facility, hire a bunch of employees, and become a manager...and neither of those visions worked for me at this point in my life. It sounded great as a plan off in the future, but it didn't work for me now.

—Andreea Ayers, Launch Grow Joy

Make sure you set some annual goals, both personal and professional. Revisit them every few months, and don't be afraid to change them if they don't make sense anymore. But if they do, make sure most of what you're doing is in some way, big or small, getting you closer to that goal.

Evaluate opportunities using your "goal filter" and don't be afraid to turn down work that doesn't fit.
          —Kathy Buckworth, KathyBuckworth.com

The Path to Success

One of the most common complaints we hear from mom entrepreneurs is that they have spent so much time and put forth so much effort only to realize that they've created a business and a life they aren't all that thrilled with. Things like societal norms, traditions, and your mindset, including making up your own set of rules that you just *have* to follow, can easily take over and dictate what you think success is supposed to look like. Before you have a chance to realize it, you can let those things guide you down a path that isn't the one you ultimately want to be on. Years go by. One day you wake up, look around you, and think, *This isn't how I thought it would be.* Stress and overwhelm kick in, or you feel disillusioned. That's not the road to happiness.

That was the case with Trish Morrison of MomCom. Growing up, Trish was lucky enough to have parents who encouraged her to be whatever she wanted to be, but that didn't stop her from making up rules for herself: she had to get the college degrees, climb the corporate ladder, manage people, and get ahead in business in order to be successful. "I've always been self-reliant," she told us. "Work was my top priority. Getting ahead. Moving up. But since I became a mom entrepreneur, I realize that's *so* not who I am. When I had Delilah, everything changed.

My priorities shifted. I was no longer willing to be gone 10 hours a day at a job. Some people can do it, but I couldn't. When she came into my life, I was all in. There was no more just me being who I wanted to be with a singular focus on myself. That all fell by the wayside!"

She had an event planning background, so Trish thought it made sense to organize a conference that would help moms connect with each other. She told us, "My vision of success back then was to have women come, listen to the awesome speakers, and have the experience change them somehow. I considered myself successful just hosting the event, getting excellent speakers who could tell a good story, and getting enough butts in the seats to cover the cost of the event. Oh, and did I make them cry? If so, then I definitely succeeded!" That vision soon morphed into a bigger (and, in hindsight, unreasonable) goal of being all things to all mothers: a Website, an online and offline community, monthly events, and franchises across the country in addition to the annual conference. She gave that vision her best shot, took some huge personal, professional, and financial risks, experienced some setbacks, and learned valuable lessons in the process. But along the way she lost sight of her original purpose and her priorities: to create a business that allowed her to spend more time with her family, and to bring moms together to hear each other's stories. While she was trying to be all things to all moms, she was working around the clock, eating, sleeping, and breathing her business. She didn't have enough time to spend with her family. The business took over every aspect of her life. "And that went against all the reasons I created MomCom in the first place," Trish told us.

This cautionary tale is similar to others we've heard from mom entrepreneurs who decided to start their own companies so they could have all the freedom, flexibility, and fulfillment that being your own boss allows. But if your metric for success doesn't align with your personal definition of success, it's pretty likely you'll wind up working just as hard for yourself as you ever did working for someone else. Before you know it, your career can take over your entire life, and we're guessing that's the opposite of what you want.

Find a job you love and you'll never work a day in your life.
—Henry Ford

Although it might have been tempting to quit or give up her business goals when she realized how far off track she was, Trish instead made the effort to figure out what success really meant to her. This clarity gave her the motivation she needed to revise her business model to one that allowed her to be professionally successful without sacrificing her commitment to put her family first. These days she's living a vision of success that makes her happy. "Now that I think of it," she told us, "I'm back to my original definition of success, which is just doing what I do best: running the conference so that moms can gather and be inspired through other moms' stories. But, now I'm clear that I also want to be paid well for it, and I have to find ways to make money without being gone from my family so much that they forget what I look like."

Trish's story illustrates that success can look different at different times, and that as you grow and evolve as a woman and a business owner, your vision of success will also evolve. The thing to keep in mind is that your sense of satisfaction and fulfillment will always be a direct reflection of how clearly you determine what you want and how closely you are following a plan to achieve it. You may have started out with a Plan A and then moved on to Plan B—or a whole bunch of other letters in the alphabet—for your company, and that's okay as long as your vision guided your choices.

Moms Talk

My idea of success has evolved quite a bit over the years...people talk about Plan B, but I feel like this is Plan Q! At first, I thought I wanted to have a successful coaching practice, but mom coaching had become a crowded space, and as my kids got older, I felt like I had outgrown the subject matter. I started creating videos, inspired mostly by my client work—my coaching clients were no longer asking how to achieve balance or how to find life purpose, but how to sync their calendar with their husband's, how to back up their contacts, or what to do with the gazillion digital photos they had on their smartphones. Once I started creating videos, I was smitten—here was a way to "coach" a massive audience, and explore new topics and territory. Digitwirl, my tech-made-easy video series, was born, and I was now a coach-turned-video-producer.

I thought Digitwirl was going to be a business I could grow, and I set out with a business plan and a dream to fund it. I was very naïve about what it would take to make that happen, and got some tough feedback (and no checks). But the concept was a success in ways I hadn't expected—all that time I spent in front of the camera teaching others how to master their technology paid off, and opportunities for TV appearances that showcased my expertise came rolling in. I made my first appearance on the Today Show in 2012, and now I'm a regular contributor. I also attracted the attention of big brands who wanted help telling their story to an audience of busy women/moms, as well as the folks at HGTV.com, who eventually signed me as digital talent and their "smart home expert."

I didn't know exactly what success looked like when I started this journey. I still don't, but most days I surrender to the not-knowing and try not to be so hard on myself! At the core of all the hats I've worn—life coach, mom coach, blogger, video producer, on-air host, smart home expert, digital lifestyle expert—is a desire to explore what I'm curious about, and share what I've learned. At every turn, my family have been involved, invested, and my biggest supporters. Conversely,

I've had to make sure that things didn't fall apart at home, and I think so far I've kept the boat from sinking, and taught my kids what it means to pursue your passion, in any form, along the way. I didn't know exactly where I was headed, and it really has changed a number of times, but I wouldn't trade the jagged path for the world.

—Carley Knobloch, Carley K

Lara suffered for a long time before realizing her vision of success wasn't working for her. While Trish's goals became clearer to her in time, Lara simply forgot to update her own vision of success. That outdated vision left her feeling like a failure once she became a mother (and, later, an entrepreneur). Prior to motherhood, Lara defined success this way:

- ✎ Working long hours
- ✎ Making a lot of money
- ✎ Traveling constantly for business and pleasure
- ✎ Being able to buy the stuff she wanted, when she wanted it
- ✎ Having a nice car
- ✎ Owning a nice house
- ✎ Dating and then eventually marrying a super guy
- ✎ Completing and delivering a big project at work
- ✎ Moving up the corporate ladder

✎ Receiving rewards, promotions, and acknowledgement from her coworkers, bosses, and
clients

Now that she's a mom, that list looks a lot different.
It took her a long time to realize that her old definition
of success simply didn't work when she applied it to her
new role of mother (and, later, to her role as a mom entrepreneur). She was frustrated, sad, angry, and resentful
because there was no one around to give her the praise and
acknowledgement she wanted for her new work—mother-
ing. "I loved my baby with all my heart. But I hated being
a mother," Lara remembers.

Her Mondays looked just like her Thursdays which
looked a lot like her Sundays, and there was no clear way
for her to judge her progress or achievements as a mom,
other than how far she had managed to get through the
mountain of dirty laundry each day. Talk about a useless
metric. The strengths and talents she had honed all her
life were a blur from her past, and although she didn't realize it at the time, not getting to use her talents was a big
source of the post-partum depression she suffered. And
she certainly didn't make any money at this new job as a
mom; in fact, she felt a huge loss of power when she no
longer earned an income herself, something she had done
consistently since she was 12 years old.

When she tried to apply her old definition of success to
her new coaching business, again, she failed miserably. She
wasn't making anywhere near the money she had made
working at IBM, she struggled to find clients, and only a
few of the clients she was working with felt like a perfect

fit. She was certain she could figure out how to solve her business problems if only she wasn't always so busy being a mother. Her frustrations were seriously impacting her business success, and she felt trapped, unhappy, and exhausted. Working for herself while trying to raise a family wasn't making her feel successful at all.

With the help of her husband and her coach, Lara learned that the definition she was using to measure her success and to feel satisfied with the life she was creating fit her about as well as a size 5 shoe. (She wears a size 10.) Her way of assessing herself and her work was outdated and no longer applicable to her life. It took some time, but knowing that, she began to *true things up* for herself. She got to work and learned how to redefine success on her own terms, starting with getting a clear understanding of her core values and priorities (which we discussed in Chapter 1). Here's how Lara now defines success for herself:

- Being healthy and taking care of myself
- Having children who are well-adjusted, confident, friendly, and compassionate, and who know how much they are loved
- Being committed to my husband and a strong, satisfying marriage
- Being loved, supported, and appreciated by my family, friends, and clients
- Doing work that fuels my passion and totally satisfies my creativity, ambition, and natural talents

- Having an income that affords our family opportunities we otherwise wouldn't have
- Doing work that makes a difference in the lives of others
- Having clients who inspire me
- Being responsible for my own happiness

So, how can you craft a vision of your successful self that will inspire you to achieve it? With a bit of time and focused intention, it's not hard to do. Consider for a moment what exactly will make you feel successful. What is it about your desired future that makes you excited to work for it? Is it the things you'd like to own, the lifestyle you'd like to live, the experiences you'd like to have, or the things you'd like to accomplish? Remember, your vision of success has to motivate you. When Andreea Ayers was considering what it meant for her to "make it big" with her soap company, she considered different ways to make the company more profitable. "I could have raised my prices on the soaps by 50 percent," she told us, "but that would have put me in a totally different market with a brand-new audience, and I just wasn't as excited about selling to my new audience as I am about selling to my current one. And I have to be super excited about what I'm doing. Otherwise, why do it?" If your vision of success doesn't get you fired up, well, we certainly don't see how you can call that success.

A note here about your mindset: If you're starting to hear those little voices inside your head telling you all the reasons why your vision of success isn't possible, don't worry. You're not alone. We all hear those voices. The act of dreaming big and thinking about what you really want for your life makes those voices loud and clear. That's just fear doing its job of trying to help you stay safe, avoid risk, and play small. So before you automatically start limiting yourself, we'd like to say, it's not too late, you aren't too old, it's not too selfish, and you aren't too busy. If you choose to let fear create your vision of success for you, well, you'll end up in a place that isn't at all what you want. So, notice the fear, trust yourself, and get going envisioning the life you deserve.

> *Fear is at the root of so many of the barriers that women face. Fear of not being liked. Fear of making the wrong choice. Fear of drawing negative attention. Fear of overreaching. Fear of being judged. Fear of failure. And the holy trinity of fear: the fear of being a bad mother/wife/daughter.*
> —Sheryl Sandberg, *Lean In*

Taking time to complete the exercises in this chapter will help you design both your business and your life in a way that meshes with all you uncovered in Chapter 1 and all that you want for yourself and your family. It will ensure that you are creating a business that is aligned with the life you dream of. The really great news is that by thoughtfully articulating and then working toward your own definition of success, you are much more likely to achieve it—and feel great when you do.

Admittedly, crafting your own version of success can be a complex endeavor when you consider all of the factors that must be included. The following graphic shows some of the factors that you'll want to keep in mind.

Your Vision of Success

This exercise will position your business vision smack in the middle of the vision for your whole life, which, for a mom entrepreneur, is the only way to make it all work. By taking the time to clarify your success criteria, you'll save yourself time and effort, not to mention the potential heartbreak that can happen when you've let someone or something else decide what it makes sense for you to work toward. Grab that sheet of paper and get ready to record your thoughts. Write the following bolded questions on your paper and leave some space to answer them, plus the supporting questions underneath. You'll want to write the bolded questions down first and then come back to each one to record your answers.

Question #1: When thinking about your business, how far into the future can you see it?

Is it three years from now? Five years? Write down a date; be specific if you can.

Now, picture yourself on that date, whenever it is. Imagine that on that date, you are wildly successful. Remember, this is a visioning exercise, so don't worry about the details or how you will reach this level of success. Suspend reality for a few minutes and just know that at that point in the future you are proud, happy, and grateful for all you've achieved.

Question #2: Looking back over the past, between your future date of success and now, what has made you so successful?

What factors have played into your success? Describe your mindset during that time of progress. What does success feel like for you? How would you describe it to someone else?

Question #3: Describe your lifestyle.

When your close friends and family are asked to describe the lifestyle that is so satisfying to you, what would they say? Where do you live? How is your health? How much time do you spend with your family, your friends, or alone for quality "me time"? How are your finances? How many hours a week do you work? How often do you take time off? What's your favorite way to spend your free time, and how do you fit it in? Answer the questions that seem most important and omit any that don't resonate for you.

Question #4: How do you spend the majority of the time in your business?

What roles do you fill in your business? What do you most enjoy doing? What do you do best? What's easiest? What makes the most money or profit for the company?

Question #5: Looking back, what are three to five key milestones that led to your success?

Think of the highlights, the points at which you did something that created opportunities that didn't exist or weren't likely to happen before. These are usually those places that felt exciting, new, and/or challenging. (By the way, does this feel a little bit like business planning? Well, you're on to us! In Chapter 6, we will be bringing these details into your business plan and building a bridge to get from your ideas to your reality.)

Question #6: What were the key growth changes/mindset shifts that supported this success?

As Henry Ford wisely said, "Whether you think you can or think you can't, you're right." Were there some limiting beliefs that you let go of? Did you notice that fear was whispering in your ear, but you decided to ignore it? Did you learn something new along the way that changed how you felt about yourself and what was possible? Or, did you acquire new skills or resources that improved your game? Did someone help you or enable you believe in yourself? Write down what comes to mind.

Question #7: What did you get from this visioning process? Did you have any "ah-ha" moments?

To get the most from this do-it-yourself coaching book, it's important for you to notice and acknowledge your patterns and recurring thoughts and beliefs. (We will address self-talk in more detail in Chapter 4.) As you continue, we will build on the answers that you're recording, so be sure to take the time to write them down. After all, you probably don't spend a lot of time purposely examining your life. This is the place to do it!

Moms Talk

If I didn't love what I do, I would have quit a long time ago. It's the big picture that keeps me going. Even though I haven't accomplished the financial success yet, I know that if I stay true to my vision, it will all pay off in the end.

—Lara Anderson, RD Shady

Not only did I make the choice to become a mom entrepreneur, but I am a SINGLE mom entrepreneur and am completely responsible for myself financially. Sure, I could have gone back into teaching; I loved teaching first grade. But I needed the flexibility and the power to control my own schedule so I could still let "mom" be my number-one job. I wanted to drop my girls off at school, volunteer, pick them up from school, make after-school snacks—all of the things I had always valued. So of course the logical decision was to do my own thing. I had a passion for fitness, I had a following, and I had confidence. I could do this. Then the reality of what it all meant set in. Rules, regulations, licenses, taxes, LLC, employees, scheduling, marketing, advertising, planning. That was a big reality.

How will I know when I have achieved success? I'm not sure if I will ever know. Success feels like a moving target. There will always be more to do, more to offer, more places to go, and more money to make. But when I wake my girls up for school, pack their lunches, pick them up at the end of their day, and offer them a snack, I feel success- ful. That was my goal, wasn't it? I'm making enough to survive. I walk into my business every morning and smile. It's mine, all mine, and I created it.

I think that moving target of success will al- ways be moving for me. But for now, this career is providing me with exactly what I need to be the mom I want to be. My girls get the benefit of see- ing me set goals for myself and our lives as I turn this dream into a reality all on my own. As a re- sult, I am able to offer the gift that I believe I have to all of the incredible clients who support me.

—Susan Slater Cotter, Strength Studio

• • •

At its heart, this chapter is really asking, "Who do you want to be?" It's worth taking some time to answer that question because who you want to be affects everything in your life and in your business. The day you wake up and find that you have the life you've been striving for and that you are the person you want to be is a very good day. We're going for happy here, so let's keep discovering what will get you there.

We have one last check-in for this chapter. Wanting something badly is a good way to make sure that you will do your very best to go after it. A strong desire can help you overcome the limits we all unconsciously place on ourselves: "I'd really reach for success if I had more money, more time, more education, more support, yadda, yadda, yadda." Now that you've had a chance to envision success, go back and make sure that what you've envisioned is truly what you want and that you are ready and willing to overcome your excuses and get to work doing whatever it will take to reach your vision.

Bottom Line

✎ Your sense of satisfaction and fulfillment will always be a direct reflection of how clearly you determine what you want and how closely you are following a plan to achieve it.

✎ Be sure your vision of success is your own.

✎ Taking the time to thoughtfully answer the questions in this chapter provides the beginnings of a road map toward the success you deserve.

Chapter 3

Time Management

Ah, time. There just never seems to be enough. And yet, rather than a true lack of time, the issue is almost always how you choose to spend it. You've probably heard suggestions about the effectiveness of tracking your time to figure out where it's really going. The concept is the same one that money experts advocate for tracking your spending. The easiest way to see where your time goes is to keep track of it for a week or so by writing down what you do each day, preferably in 15-minute increments. If the refrains of your life are "I have no time" and "I don't know where the days go," or if you feel as though you are always running out of time, this is probably a very useful exercise.

Many of us already have a pretty good idea of how we spend our time. E-mails, snail mail, scheduling appointments, carpool, shopping for and making meals, exercise, and doing laundry may take up big chunks. If we are honest, Facebook, TV, and surfing the 'net likely use up more than we'd readily admit. (Did we just date ourselves? Is it still called "surfing the 'net"?) Over and over, we've heard women say time (or the lack thereof) is their biggest issue. We are here to tell you that there really is enough time to do the things you want to do. What most women could more accurately say is, "I'm spending my time in the wrong way. I'm doing things that aren't that important to me, that don't move me toward my goals, and that end up making me feel rushed or empty or frustrated." It's so easy to fall into that trap, and it's the number-one reason we walk around lamenting our lack of time.

Show us a woman working a reasonable (to her) number of hours a week toward a specific goal she has set for herself and we'll show you a woman who feels productive and exhilarated. Show us another woman working that same number of hours a week with no target, no plan, and no focus, and we'll show you a woman who feels stressed out, frustrated, and short on time. What's the difference between exhilarated and exhausted? The only difference is intentionally choosing to spend time on your priorities.

When you are running your business and managing your family, you really can't afford to aimlessly while away hours of time. And why would you want to? Reclaiming those hours could not only give you time to fit in the things you have to do but could also allow you to finally paint or run or knit or learn Spanish or, well, you get the idea. One way to think about your time is to see it as currency: You have 24 hours a day to spend. Take away the time you need to sleep, eat, run your house, get groceries, take care of your kids, and nurture your marriage or partnership if you are in one, and you'll discover the amount of time that you have left to budget for both your business and yourself. As we never tire of saying, when you are a mom entrepreneur, your priorities are your boss. Because you don't have a boss at an office telling you what to work on, let your priorities dictate your to-dos instead. They provide a framework for how to spend your time effectively. It's so easy to feel like a victim of too little time, but when you align the way you spend your time with the things that are most important to you, you begin to feel as though you have a lot more control than you are used to.

What if you could reclaim your days and use them in a way that makes you feel productive and more—dare we say the word—balanced? Did you notice that we didn't say you will *be* balanced? That's a promise we can't make because perfect balance doesn't exist for more than an instant. But *feeling* more balanced? Yes, we can help you there. First, let's look at some of the reasons you may feel short on time.

You know the saying "old habits die hard"? We are creatures of habit, and even when we know that something we do isn't being done in the most effective or the most efficient way, sometimes we just keep doing it because it's what we know. It's what feels comfortable. Think for a few minutes about some of your habits that chip away at your time. Do you always check e-mail first thing in the morning and find that when you've finished, half of the morning has been taken up by reacting to what others want you to do? (Hello, boundaries!) Or what about keeping a set lunch date with someone every Monday even though you know that it makes Monday after Monday feel unproductive and rushed? There are also seemingly harmless habits like checking Pinterest 10 times a day.

Take a few minutes to think of the habits you have that take up too much of your time. Write them down, cite the problem(s) they create, think of at least one way to break yourself of the habit, and then write down the benefit to be gained if you do.

The last step of this is probably the most important one. By articulating the benefit to be gained by changing your ways, you are more likely to adapt your behavior. Here's an example:

Habit: I put my phone next to my desk while I'm trying to write.

Problem: I keep getting interrupted.

Way to break myself of the habit: I'll put my phone in the other room instead.

Benefit: Uninterrupted writing time.

You must have at least one habit that isn't serving you, so here's your chance to remedy that.

Our choices lead to another major time drain. How often do you automatically say yes when someone asks you to do something? Every time you say yes to something, you are giving away your time. Sometimes that's exactly the right thing for you to do. Saying yes to something you are excited about or to something that you really want to do, even if it's not that exciting, is great. But keep in mind that each yes means saying no to something else. Think about that. Saying yes to helping with the school auction could mean saying no to something else that is even more important or more meaningful. Luckily, you've gotten clear on your priorities, and referring back to them will help you decide which things are a yes and which things are a no. And *no* doesn't have to be *no forever*, because sometimes you have to say no to something that is important and that will eventually be a yes. Sometimes it's a no for now because the timing isn't right. Sometimes it's a no for now because you've inadvertently said yes to too many other things.

What about the "important" things that consistently slip to the bottom of your to-do list? Perhaps that's a hint that those things aren't what's most important right now. Saying "I don't have time" for something really means that you are choosing to spend your time on something else for now. And that's okay. For instance, Erin would like to learn to play the piano. You wouldn't know that, though, because she doesn't ever sit down to do it. What can she learn from that? Simple: it's not a current priority. It is important to her. She intends to do it someday. But right now, while she has school-aged children and is running a business while writing and promoting a book, piano just falls to the bottom of the list.

Moms Talk

Be aware of over-commitment. As you see success, others may call on you to volunteer (board involvement, mentorship, etc.). Realize that every time you say YES to something, you will be saying NO to something else. I run things by my husband before I say yes to volunteer opportunities. He helps me prioritize and see what I will have to remove from my schedule if I say yes to whatever is before me.

—Shannon Wilburn, Just Between Friends Consignment

Another huge factor that can contribute to your feeling that you don't have enough time is lack of planning. So many of us start the day without a real plan. We sit down to work and we don't quite know where to start. We have a huge project to get finished, we need to return some business calls, and we want to work on our marketing plan, but we haven't set a plan to do any of those things so we start by checking e-mail. We might look at Twitter. We find an article that we decide to read. We go back to e-mail and reply to a few of them. We read one that requires action on our part and, because we aren't ready to take action, we leave it in our inbox. By now, we need to go to the bathroom or get another cup of coffee. Before we know it, it's time for lunch and we've not accomplished much at all. That's when the icky feeling sets in: *What a waste of a morning. I wanted to get in some exercise. I meant to*

*call that distributor to figure out what's going wrong. And
even though I checked e-mail, I didn't respond, so they are
all still there, plus I've gotten 15 more.*

That's why it's so important to plan your time. We'll
talk more about how to do this later in the chapter, but
let's start with one simple thing we encourage everyone to
do: Get in the habit of spending a few minutes before you
finish up working for the day to make a plan for the next
day. Ideally you would map out your whole day, but even
if it's only jotting down what you want to do first thing, go
ahead and put it on your calendar. Most of us like to have
our marching orders so we can hit the ground running
without having to think too much about where to start.

Sometimes—not very often, mind you—we find ourselves with extra time. For example, a client can't make a
scheduled call or a meeting gets cancelled. That extra time
often ends up being wasted because, again, we haven't
planned for it and we aren't sure what the heck to do with
it. That's where Hit Lists come in. A Hit List is a list of
ideas on a particular topic that you've created in advance.
It's your best resource when you find yourself with time
to spend because it provides either to-dos or a list of possibilities that you can access right away. We create business
Hit Lists for non-urgent but necessary administrative jobs,
marketing tasks, and business ideas we want to try, just to
name a few. The point is to think ahead, write these lists
down, and then use them when you need them. That way,
when you arrive 15 minutes early to an appointment or
you finish a project an hour earlier than you'd planned,
you'll know what to do.

By the way, you don't have to limit Hit Lists to work-related tasks. We recommend Hit Lists as a quick way to come up with all sorts of solutions: easy dinners to make, rainy day activities to keep your kids busy, summer activities around your town, small household projects, non-urgent errands you need to run, birthday gift ideas for your kids' friends, books you want to read, books your kids might like, and family movies you want to watch. Capturing all of this information on lists will save you time and energy and will keep the ideas from swirling around endlessly in your head.

Take a look at the sample Hit List one of our clients created when she was struggling with running her company after her second child was born. We all know that babies don't understand a thing about time and don't follow the appointments we put on our calendar. It's a constant challenge to try to work at all when you have an infant nursing every couple of hours. And yet, there are things you *can* do to make some progress. Her Hit List of tasks that were aimed at boosting her presence on social media (shown on the next page) gave her quick reminders of things she could do whenever she found 15 minutes of free time. Why not make a Hit List of 15-minute tasks for yourself right now?

Social Media Hit List

- find and follow relevant social media users
- retweet new followers
- content for site and social media:
  - post ideas
  - images
  - tweets
  - pins
  - quotes
- monthly theme for next quarter
- research prospective clients
- find content for our followers
- schedule tweets and posts for next day or two

Now let's talk about boundaries. *Boundaries* is a term therapists often use to help their patients teach others how to treat them. Using boundaries is a way to make sure that the way people speak to you and interact with you match up with what is tolerable to you. We are going to talk about boundaries more in terms of managing your time, but the idea is similar. We're going to encourage you to become comfortable with boundaries because it's up to you to make sure yours are protected. Creating boundaries can sometimes seem selfish or silly or (fill in the blank with another word that will make you less likely to enforce them). But here's the thing: sticking with the boundaries having to do with your time lets you more easily accomplish all that you are setting out to do. And guess what? Sometimes, when it comes to boundaries, you will be protecting yourself from *you!*

Moms Talk

I work at home, which I absolutely love. At first it was hard because I was distracted by all of the household chores that needed to be done. The best thing I've done recently is hire a cleaning service and establish regular office hours when my clients know for sure they can reach me. I try to be available for urgent issues outside of those hours, but I found that being at their beck and call during my waking hours, 6 a.m. to 10 p.m., is exhausting and not sustainable. When I stick to my office hours, my life seems to run more smoothly. I make exercise and meditation a priority every day, before I start my office hours, if possible. I need to fill my cup before I can be of service to others.

I don't regret for a minute leaving my great corporate job in the pursuit of "having it all." It's taken a lot more time—and work—to find that balance I was looking for, but I feel like I've got it.

—Amy Anderson, Fleurish Partners

Here's an example that comes up time and again with our clients—and we'll admit it, with us too. Let's say you know you have six hours to work on Wednesday between all of the other activities on your calendar. Six hours is a lot of time if you are really focused and productive. Six hours is not a lot of time if, during those hours, you are also doing laundry, catching up on personal e-mails, and accepting phone calls from friends. When it comes to boundaries, you really need to make a promise to yourself that work time is work time. Likewise, if you want 5 to 9 p.m. to be family time, make sure that you aren't answering work e-mails or scheduling work calls during that time. We'll cover this a bit more in Chapter 7 but for now, think about how you let others and yourself cross your time boundaries and steal precious time away from either your work time or your personal time. Take a few minutes to write down the common culprits or situations as well as solutions for them.

For instance, if your children interrupt you when you're working, setting up some ground rules and consequences or rewards around that is a way to overcome the interruptions. Or, if you can't be trusted to stay off social media during the time you are supposed to be making sales calls, closing your browser and disabling alerts would be good solutions.

Lack of time is actually lack of priorities.
—Tim Ferris

In her book, *168 Hours: You Have More Time Than You Think*, Laura Vanderkam writes about everyone having the same 168 hours each week. She suggests that it's not that we have too little time but that we don't allot our time in a way that would allow us to get done the things we really want to get done.[1] It all goes back to what we've talked about: priorities. As a mom entrepreneur, your priorities need to dictate how you spend your 168 hours. (Do we sound like a broken record yet?) That said, taking ownership of your time is sometimes easier said than done. It means breaking old habits, making good choices, setting boundaries, thoughtfully scheduling your time, and really honoring what is most important to you.

Moms Talk

For me, priority number one is to keep all the living things in our house alive via healthy food and hydration: kids, dogs, birds, and adults all get fed. Priority number two: stick to the business plan so that meetings, marketing, and communication all happen according to the schedule I set each week. Anything else after these two things falls into categories three and below. Painting the house trim and weeding the garden? I think those might qualify as priority numbers 47 and 48, respectively. It takes perseverance to maintain devotion to items one and two; all the rest of the flotsam will want to creep in and take control, but truthfully, the dusting can wait.

On occasion, I do want to crawl under my desk chair and hide. My home phone rings consistently throughout the day, the general assumption being that if I'm in the house, I'm not actually working. I am asked, on a regular basis, to volunteer, chaperone, and attend various functions at my children's schools. I notice my husband does not receive such invitations, but then again, people perceive his time constraints as more legitimate because he works outside the home. Whereas I make an attempt to regularly participate at both children's schools, I've learned to not say yes to everything lest I give away the most precious part of my day: the time during which I create. Without time to create, I have—I am—nothing.

—Michelle Ciarlo-Hayes, MKC Photography

I couldn't do everything I wanted to do, so one of the hardest things for me was picking and choosing priorities and being okay with that. And realizing our limitations, and not looking at what other people were doing, but looking at what we could do. When you have a great idea, you want to run with it. And in our case, we really couldn't run with it, because we were limited with time, with money, and with energy. It just takes so much out of you to start your own business that we were tapped on all levels. So we took it as we could. And we fought our guilt or our "I wish we could do this, I wish we could do that." We had to keep it in perspective.

—Becky Harper, ReUsies

Once I realized that I was not at the mercy of time, and that to some extent I controlled it, things became much easier. The fact is if we tell ourselves "I have no time" and "I can't get it all done," what we're actually doing is affirming that to ourselves. If we start singing a different tune, we'll find time does the same. Start telling yourself every morning, "I have plenty of time today to do everything I want to do," or "Time is on my side," or "There's always plenty of time." The trick is not to panic, and not to let it get the better of you.

—Michelle Dale, Virtual Miss Friday

I've never been able to fit it all in. One day your toilet is clean and the next day all your e-mails are returned. This is my balance.

—Terry Grahl, Enchanted Makeovers

Knowing that you can choose differently and design your time in a way that will work for you, let's do a simple exercise to figure out if how you spend your time matches up with your priorities. In just a few minutes of work, you'll know where your time and priorities are in sync and where they aren't. Get out your pen and paper.

Here is a sample:

Priorities:	How I spend my time:
	- exercising
	- marketing
1. Family	- networking events
	- carpooling
	- errands
2. Health	- volunteering at school
	- housekeeping
	- lunch/brunch with friends
3. Marriage	- client meetings
	- bookkeeping
	- making meals
4. Business	- homework with kids
	- planning meals
	- grocery shopping
	- house projects
	- emails

As in the graphic, you'll want to create two columns. On the left side of your paper, write down your four priorities from Chapter 1. On the right side, list all of the ways you spend your time. For now, it's most useful to look at the major chunks of time rather than writing down every tiny detail of your day. Your list may include some of the items you see on the sample, so look at that for ideas. Be sure to include all of your regular commitments. Now, draw a line from each activity to the priority or priorities that the activity supports. For instance, if you listed *health* as a priority on the left and *exercise* on the right, draw a line to connect them. Or, if you listed a priority of *financial stability* on the left and *work* on the right, you may be able to connect those, assuming that your work brings in enough income to increase your financial stability.

Once you've had a chance to complete the exercise, you'll likely find that you need to make some adjustments. Notice which of your activities are not connected by a line to one of your priorities. Those are the things you do that don't support your priorities. Make a note of them. Next, notice if there are priorities that are not supported by activities that routinely show up on your schedule. Jot those items down as well. Next, think about changes you might need to make so that you can spend your time in a way that better matches with the things that are most important to you.

On the sample we provided, you'll see that *marriage* is listed as a priority but there aren't any activities that directly support that priority. Perhaps the person whose list this is could add a weekly date night to her schedule. She is doing several things that support her priority of family: carpooling, volunteering at school, homework with kids, and shopping, planning, and making meals, so that priority is sufficiently taken care of by those activities.

When we were writing this book, getting it done so we could get it into your hands was a huge priority. However, you wouldn't have known that by the meager amount of time we sometimes spent working on it. Heeding our own advice, we adjusted our activities (the way we spent our time) to include many more book-related tasks, which then matched up nicely with our priority of finishing the book. Suddenly, we were saying yes to writing the book and no to other things that seemed interesting or exciting but that took time away from writing.

Calendaring

Now that you have a better idea of the activities you should continue doing, what you need to add, and what you need to eliminate or minimize, it's important to plot out your to-dos on your calendar. There are so many calendar options out there to choose from. Pick the one that you are actually going to use. If that's an old-fashioned paper planner, use that. If it's a Web-based calendar that the whole family can access, fine. Mobile calendar apps are handy because most of us keep our phones with us at all times. Just pick one that works for you and stick with it.

The easiest way for most people to start is to put in the recurring events they know about. So, if your son has soccer practice every Tuesday and Thursday from 3 to 5 p.m., put that on your calendar. Most of us have a fairly standard morning routine; for example, Lara blocks off 7 to 9 a.m. Monday through Friday to feed herself and her kids, prep lunches, and get the kids to school. (See examples of her daily and weekly calendars on the next two pages.) Get all recurring events on your calendar before moving on.

The next phase of calendaring is adding in the tasks you have to do. These are the tasks that are non-negotiable, and they will be unique to you. You might say that exercise

Lara's Daily Calendar

7am - 9am	wake up, morning routine, take kids to school
9am - 10am	run
10am - 4pm	work
4pm - 7pm	kids arrive home from school, close computer, quality time, homework help, dinner prep and eat
7pm - 9pm	kitchen clean up, laundry, household chores, prep for next day
9pm - 11pm	hubby time, occasional work project time

is a non-negotiable. Get it on your calendar, then. Time to work is a likely one, because if you are this far into this book you probably own a business or are about to start one. Refer back to your priorities if you need help coming up with some of your non-negotiables. And because our schedules are often built around our children's schedules, consider how the end of the school day, extracurricular activities, and helping with homework fit into your daily routine.

Another non-negotiable we like to put in right away is the time that we will sign off for the night. It may seem

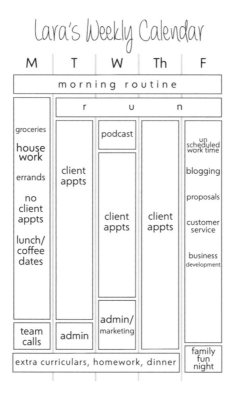

Lara's Weekly Calendar

M	T	W	Th	F
morning routine				
	r	u	n	
groceries		podcast		unscheduled work time
house work	client appts			blogging
errands				proposals
no client appts		client appts	client appts	customer service
lunch/ coffee dates				business development
		admin/ marketing		
team calls	admin			family fun night
extra curriculars, homework, dinner				

ludicrous that you'd have to schedule the end of your work day, but if your calendar says that your work time ends at 9 p.m., you'll probably allow yourself to be done with work by 9 p.m. Funny little creatures, aren't we?

Now that you've plotted out the most important tasks and activities and the ones that are already scheduled, how do you decide what else shows up on your calendar? Here are some criteria you can use to help you decide whether or not something deserves a spot.

- ✎ Does it honor my priorities?
- ✎ Is it part of a plan I've already made?

- ✎ Is it something I really want to do?
- ✎ Is it something that moves me toward my goals?
- ✎ Is it part of my self-care routine?
- ✎ Does it use my strengths and/or am I looking forward to doing it?

You can even use the tool we talked about earlier. *By putting* this *on my calendar* (saying yes), *I'm saying no to* that. With the tools we're teaching, your calendar should now reflect all that's important to you as well as actions that will lead you toward all that you want.

When you are plotting out your calendar, be sure to pay attention to what you know about yourself and your energy levels. For instance, if you know that you get sleepy around noon, don't schedule a hardcore workout during that time. Or if your mind starts wandering around 3 p.m., that's probably not the time to attempt to solve a big issue that's been nagging you. Some people feel their most energized in the morning so they hit the ground running and take care of the most important tasks on their lists first thing. Other people need a bit of time to wake up first so they go through e-mail and read the paper before launching their day. Make your calendar work for you by scheduling yourself in a way that works best for you. (We even know one mom who works late into the night, gets up to help her kids in the morning, and then naps once they are off to school.)

Speaking of energy and natural rhythms, remember to build some down time into your calendar. In *The Power of Full Engagement*, Jim Loehr and Tony Schwartz illustrate that managing energy, rather than time, is actually the key to a productive, fulfilling, and successful life.[2] In their book, they demonstrate how our energy ebbs and flows and why it's crucial to acknowledge and honor that. We are not built to work 12 hours straight. Some people can toil away for hours and hours without a break, but we have to think that those of you who can do that are the exception. There is nothing wrong with taking some time for yourself—in fact, it's essential for your self-care, as you'll see in Chapter 4. The problem arises when we create a conflict for ourselves by not scheduling in the down time we need. In that case, we are likely to revolt. Suddenly, when we have set aside two hours to spend working, we'll find ourselves guiltily reading a magazine or browsing Pinterest. What do we do next? We berate ourselves for being lazy or off task, of course. It's a cycle we recommend you avoid by leaving time on your schedule for breaks.

The important thing is to know how you function best and to build the necessary breaks into your schedule. You need to be really honest with yourself about your need to recharge. We'll talk about this more when we talk about self-care, but just know that you will need down time here and there, so don't schedule your days with back-to-back-to-back activities if you can help it. And, just to catch those of you who are looking for loopholes to sabotage yourself: Building in breaks is not an excuse to browse the Internet or check your e-mail every 10 minutes. We are not giving you permission to lounge the day away on the couch, either. What we are saying is that each of us has our own biorhythms that control when we can do certain types of work, and it's fairly easy to figure out what they are.

To make sure we are using our time well while also acknowledging our needs for breaks, we like to reward ourselves for our hard work. Did you work hard all morning, accomplishing intentional to-dos? Let yourself spend lunch poring over a book or magazine that you've been looking forward to reading. Or do whatever it is that you love to do.

Schedule time to work, time to exercise, time to relax, and time for whatever other activities make up your life, including date nights, errands, and phone calls with friends to catch up. If there is a place for it on your calendar, it's much more likely to happen. And while we are on the subject, really honor the items on your calendar and therefore yourself. Make your fun appointments just as significant as your work appointments. Schedule them and keep them.

Here is one last tip for you when it comes to scheduling. Even though we just said to honor your calendar commitments, we do know that life sometimes gets in the way. To help remedy this, consider *overscheduling* yourself for some tasks. By that we mean, put them on your calendar several times. For instance, if you want to work out three times a week, put it on your calendar five times. If you need to run some errands, schedule it during several different open times during the week so that if something gets in your way the first time it's scheduled, you can actually do it the next time it shows up. It's a trick we learned a while back. Try it to see if it works for you too.

Finding More Time

Let's talk about ways to find more time. Of course, you can't really find more time, because, as we mentioned, we all have the same 168 hours each week. That said, there are ways to seemingly make time stretch. Most of these are not meant to be used on a long-term basis, but we all have occasional projects and deadlines that take an extra push to finish. If you find yourself needing to make the day seem longer so you can accomplish something in the short term, here is our list of ways to do that. We bet you can come up with others as well.

- Get up earlier
- Stay up later
- Let some things go for now (reading the newspaper, chatting with neighbors, Facebook)
- Get singularly focused on whatever needs to be accomplished (limit multitasking and transitions from one task to another)
- Delegate
- Hire a temporary VA (virtual assistant) or intern
- Ask for help

• • •

Managing your time may require a shift in thinking or it may require some bigger shifts in boundaries and choices. The idea is to take control of how you spend your days so that you can create a life that makes you happy and fulfilled. If you make any necessary changes and still find that time doesn't seem to be on your side, we have a suggestion for you: Rather than beat yourself up day after day over the things that you did not get done, acknowledge that you are one person, that you can only do so much, that you are likely accomplishing quite a lot, that your days are full, that you need and are entitled to breaks and fun and time to do nothing, and that you are doing the best you can. The to-do list will never go away, so instead of entering into a 50-year abusive conversation with yourself, maybe you could shift your thinking and give yourself a nice little pat on the back at the end of each day for a job well done. Sometimes that simple act of surrender to *what is* will be enough to shift things so you can end each day feeling accomplished.

We can strive to get smarter and more efficient about how we use and spend our time, but it's always going to be a challenge to manage it. That's just par for the course. Part of the challenge is a natural one given our lifestyle as mom, wife, neighbor, business owner, and so forth. But the other part is that our society seems to reward busyness. These days it's almost as though people have entered into a competition to see who is the busiest. We want you to know that *busy* does not equal *important* or *worthwhile* or *valuable*. There is no prize for being the busiest. So set your sights on accomplishing the things that are most important to you. Take care of the things that have to be done. And then use at least some of the time that's left over to play, to relax, or simply to be.

Bottom Line

- Good time management starts with taking orders from your boss: your priorities.

- Spending time on the things that are most important to you will make you feel as though you have the time you need.

- To make the most of your time, you may need to break some old habits and create some new ones.

- Some planning and scheduling go a long way toward making sure the most important stuff gets done.

- Using Hit Lists for quick tasks that you can do when you find "extra" time in your day can make you even more productive.

- Remember to schedule breaks and rewards into your day.

Chapter 4

Self-Care

You're a mom entrepreneur. You have at least two full-time jobs: running a family and running a business. The potential for burnout is high, but we want something better for you. Because this is a marathon and not a sprint, you're going to need to take really good care of yourself along the way. This chapter is dedicated to just that.

What exactly is self-care? It's just what it sounds like: taking good care of yourself. Simple, right? And, yet so many of us don't do it. Often, it's much more complicated than it needs to be because of the guilt that surrounds it, because we are so often pressed for time, because of the comparisons we tend to make, and because acts of self-care can feel downright selfish. We're going to help you find a way to fit it in, though, because it might just be the most important part of your path to success.

The kind of self-care we're talking about starts with acknowledging (and embracing) the fact that you have your own needs and wants that are often separate from, and different than, those of your family. And, while you are likely good at anticipating, managing, and handling the needs and wants of others, there is a chance that when it comes to your own needs and wants, you are not as skilled. Somehow, the things that will really fuel you and give you the energy that you need to thrive, slip to the bottom of your to-do list. And, likely, you end each day thinking about how you want tomorrow to be different.

To tempt you just a bit, here are some of the benefits of good self-care:

- ✎ Improved confidence
- ✎ Improved mental health
- ✎ Improved sleep
- ✎ Improved overall sense of well-being
- ✎ Improved productivity
- ✎ Improved ability to deal with stress

Compelling, right? Still, part of the reason we put off caring for ourselves is that many women feel that self-care is something they need to earn. How would we earn it? Likely by finishing our neverending to-do lists—which we know will never happen. See how we set it up so that self-care is always at the bottom of our lists? What if you knew that taking great care of yourself was essential to being the best possible version of yourself? What if you knew that self-care was one of the key ingredients to creating the success you crave? And what if your company's bottom line depended on it? After all, taking great care of yourself gives you a strong foundation from which to accomplish all that you are setting out to do.

If you're going to embark on or continue this monumental task of owning a business while raising a family, you're going to need to get really good at self-care. If you don't, you could actually be setting yourself up to fail. On the other hand, regularly doing things that replenish and refuel you is a surefire way to have the energy and stamina you'll need to reach your goals.

Good self-care is critical to making sure that you don't burn out. Over and over again, we've seen some type of burnout with our clients. Picture this: You get into a productive cycle with your business and it's paying off, so you decide to work more hours so you can move toward what you want and get more positive results quickly. Soon, you begin to forego exercise, eat crappy food, and go to bed too late. Or you let e-mails pile up, and the snail mail starts to accumulate too. And so much for keeping in touch with friends or hanging out with your family. There just isn't time. We can all sustain this go-go-go lifestyle for a short time, but guess what happens when you try to live like that for more than a few days? You burn out. You realize what a mess you've made and you retreat into a slump. You feel sorry for yourself and take this opportunity to bemoan the unfair nature of life. Give it some time and you begin to regain your mojo. You emerge again, restore your equilibrium, and get your life back on track. And then, rather than learning from past mistakes, you start the whole cycle (or a very similar one) again. We've all been there, but here's the thing: taking good care of yourself prevents you from going down this road in the first place.

If you don't give yourself time to recharge, you are sabotaging yourself. It's a strong word but it's the truth. Plus, you are sending yourself the message that you aren't important enough to nurture. You can push yourself to the limit for a short while, and sometimes you just don't have much of a choice, but it's not a sustainable way to live. If you rarely make time to recharge, it truly is a form of self-sabotage, whether it's conscious or not. And, if you don't make time for self-care, things will eventually bite you in the butt. (That is not the technical term or the scientifically correct way to describe what happens, but we hope you get the picture.) Remember, as the CEO of your business, you're modeling the behavior you expect from your team. And as the CEO of your family, you're modeling the behavior you expect to see from your kids. Don't you want them to learn to take good care of themselves? By the way, you'll know you need to take better care of yourself because you and your family will start to see the signs. If you are crabby, resentful, short-tempered, or easily prone to tears, you might want to consider these warning signs that you need to crank your self-care up a notch or two. (Or else, maybe you need to take a pregnancy test?)

On a related note, we have come to the realization that there really is no way to achieve the media-hyped ideal of balance in your life—at least not for more than a passing moment. What you can do, though, is regularly take some time to determine whether you are moving toward balance or away from it. You'll know the answer to that question without having to give it much thought. Have you found yourself in a constant hurry lately? Is "breakfast for dinner" becoming a habit? Have your kids complained that they are out of clean clothes? Do you wish you could stop the world for a day or two to catch up? If so, you are likely moving away from balance.

Moms Talk

When I started my business, I tried to think strategically about what I could do on a daily basis...spiritually, emotionally, and physically. I wasn't sure how to measure the kind of balance I was seeking, but I knew what imbalance felt like, so by trial and error I figured out exactly the kind of work that I wanted to do.

—Sue Anne Morgan, Idealand

When you start to feel as though life is running you ragged, it's time to stop and check in. It won't always be self-care that's missing, but we're willing to bet that if you're feeling frazzled, that's a good place to look. Luckily, you are about to create a Hit List of self-care items that you can refer to when you start noticing that something is off. **Hint:** In the future, if you look at your list and notice that you haven't done anything on it for a long time, you'll want to make the time to fit in some self-care. It's counterintuitive to take time for an activity that feels luxurious when you barely have time to get to the grocery store, but we promise it's often the first step forward toward a happier and more productive you.

Moms Talk

I know that when things start spiraling out of control and I find my shoulders in my ears and a snippy tone in my voice, I need to take a step back and breathe. I need to stop and look at my life and see what exactly is out of whack.

—Kathryn Cree Bouchard, Tweak

How do we incorporate a healthy ritual of self-care into our daily lives? We all need the basics: healthy food, plenty of sleep, and exercise. These are the bare minimum, and if you aren't getting them, it's time to add them to your schedule. Seriously, like right now. Go on a walk. Grab an apple. And if you're reading this at one in the morning, as much as we hate to tell you to put this book down, it's time to go to bed. We'll be here waiting when you've had some sleep. If the three basics aren't there in your life, that's a huge red flag that we encourage you to pay attention to. Just as you wouldn't expect a plant to grow if you didn't water it, or your car to run if you did't fill up the gas tank, going about your business without the basics of food, exercise, and sleep is asking the impossible of yourself. You certainly wouldn't allow your kids to go without food or sleep, so why would you deny yourself of these basics?

Your Plan

Let's get specific on the other things—aside from food, exercise, and sleep—you need for good self-care. (Note that by *you* we mean not the collective *you* but *you*, the person reading this right now). In the game of self-care, all you really have to do is determine the things that make you feel great and then incorporate them into your days. Common activities include reading, yoga, meditation, crossword puzzles, walks, exercise, and coffee with friends. There are no wrong answers here as long as the things you list refuel you or relax you—or both. Ideally, your list will include some stress relievers, some activities that make you feel pampered, some things that are pure fun, and at least a couple that involve laughing. After all, according to researchers, laughter reduces stress, improves your ability to solve problems, and increases both your self-esteem and your resilience.

And, while you are making your list, may we suggest adding in some "twofers"? Twofers are activities that help you kill two birds with one stone. Reading your favorite magazine while getting a pedicure is an example. Other examples are going to yoga with your daughter or going on a walk with a friend who makes you laugh. Lara's favorite includes running on the treadmill while watching reruns of *Project Runway* or listening to podcasts while she jogs around the neighborhood.

Moms Talk

I have to be honest: I don't have a lot of time for self-care. I get my hair cut twice a year and you don't want to know the last time I got a wax! I would like to get to the gym, but instead I go for hikes with my family and play road hockey with my tweens. This is the life I chose, and having traditional "me time" is not a priority right now.

I think self-care is important and knowing your needs is essential. I would not have had six kids and started a business if my needs were high in this area.

However, after many years of sleep deprivation, it certainly takes its toll and it is an area I've tried to improve on. My wake-up call was when I was driving down the street with a van full of my kids and I forgot where we were going. I pulled over and looked into my rearview mirror and saw a child in a soccer uniform. Ah! Soccer it is, then—off to the soccer field I went!

—Julie Cole, Mabel's Labels and parenting blogger

What are the things *you* need to do to take great care of yourself? What helps you recharge? Take a few minutes to decide what self-care means to you. Be honest. Grab your pen and paper and write down your favorite ways to take care of yourself. Don't be embarrassed if "reading *People Magazine*" shows up on your list.

We asked the mom entrepreneurs in our online communities to share their best tips for squeezing in self-care when you don't think you have the time. There were so many creative responses. We discussed in Chapter 2 how success doesn't look the same for everyone. As it turns out, neither does self-care. Some moms don't need much in the way of self-care. Others really need to spend a good amount of time on it each week in order to feel their best. Take a look at this list of some of their rechargers and see if you can swipe a couple of great ideas to keep you calm, grounded, and feeling as though you can handle everything that comes at you. Use these ideas to create your own Self-Care Hit List.

Self-Care Ideas from Fellow Mom Entrepreneurs

Book your next pedicure/ massage/hair appointment before you leave the salon	Read	Meditate just before bed
Light a candle and pour a glass of wine on your way to a hot bath	Go for a walk	Do yoga at home
Check out resources online for short, guided meditations	Take a few extra minutes in the bathroom—that locked door is effective!	Watch a TEDTalk video

Take a quick nap	Read an indulgent magazine such *People*, *Cosmo*, or *Vogue*	Go get a manicure or pedicure, or do it yourself
Call a friend or family member	Meet your husband/partner for a quick lunch	Play soccer with your kids
Do deep breathing	Take a long shower and try out a new body scrub	Give yourself a facial
Close your eyes and listen to your favorite music	Play or cuddle with your pet	Get a massage
Have a cup of coffee or tea	Do some gardening	Ask for help and get some things off your plate

Now comes what is possibly the hardest part of all: Taking the time to *do* the things we listed, guilt-free. We emphasize "guilt-free" because it's important to do these things with a sense of calm rather than the anxiety that often comes with doing something you believe you shouldn't be doing. Here's the fun part: these so-called guilty pleasures are actually good for both you *and* your business. A growing body of evidence shows that taking regular breaks from mental tasks improves productivity and creativity, and, conversely, that skipping breaks can lead to stress and exhaustion. If you think about it, what is the alternative when you need a break and you don't give it to yourself? You'll likely sit in front of your laptop hitting refresh to see if any exciting e-mails have come in rather than accomplishing anything. You may as well do something nourishing from your Hit List instead. Take a break so you can be more productive.

How do you fit these activities in when your schedule is already full? It's so easy to come up with excuses as to why you don't have time for these seemingly unproductive activities. That's why dedicating time for them is so important. Hopefully, Chapter 3 helped you get clear about how to schedule your time. If so, fitting them in could be as easy as plugging them into the time slots you left open for relaxation. If not, now is a good time to go back and rework your schedule so you have a place for the items you listed.

Moms Talk

I really like schedules, and I include personal time in mine as it is just as important as business time. Also, I accept that there are only 24 hours in a day and have reasonable expectations about what I hope to accomplish in them.

—Michelle Dale, Virtual Miss Friday

Again, having a self-care Hit List will help you know what to do if you find yourself with extra time, so why not print it out and post it as a great visual reminder to make time for yourself?

Now you have regularly scheduled self-care time on your calendar as well as a plan for unexpected time. Build the items on your list into your days and weeks, and you will reap the rewards. We also suggest taking mini mental breaks often throughout the day. Even if you just get up and walk around for 30 seconds or step outside and breathe, it's a good idea to reset here and there, either when you are making a transition from one task to another or when you've been working on something for a long time. (We know of one woman, who shall remain nameless, who sits in a stall in the ladies room at her office just to get some much-needed time alone in the middle of her work day.) Also, this seems obvious, but take time to eat when you're hungry. If you haven't eaten lunch, do you think you'll be working at your most productive level? During your personal time, it's always possible to fit in self-care while doing the things you already do: listen to music while you are doing the dishes, light a scented candle when you are about to take a shower, or lift some hand weights when you are catching up on your DVR.

It's great to build in self-nurturing things such as time with friends and family, but may we suggest that at least some of your self-care time be spent in silence? We would like to bring back a lost art the Italians call *Il dolce far niente*, or the sweetness of doing nothing. We think they are onto something. Seriously, we are such a nation of doers that we've largely lost the art of being. We don't like to tell people what to do, but if we had to make an exception, it would be to tell you to meditate. The benefits are great, you can do it just about anywhere, and it doesn't cost a dime. Taking five or 10 minutes out of your day to just *be* is like pushing a reset button. This may be the hardest assignment we give, but please consider spending some time in silence. You don't even have to try to quiet your thoughts, which is one of the major reasons people say they don't meditate. In fact, when you give yourself a chance to hear them, you can tap into some pretty incredible creative notions. Who knows? The time you spend with your thoughts just might spark your next great business idea.

We hope you'll take what we've said as your permission slip to nurture and honor yourself. For a variety of reasons, women—and moms in particular—tend to have a hard time letting ourselves rest, relax, and rejuvenate. We see it as lazy or as an unnecessary indulgence, or, as we mentioned before, we think we need to earn it. STOP THAT RIGHT NOW! Those silly ideas couldn't be further from the truth. You know your kids need down time; you encourage them to take it, because you know how much more pleasant they are to be around when they've had some. Your team also has a better perspective and is more productive after a nice break or vacation. Well, guess what? You need it too. So, even if you have to force yourself, we implore you to do it.

Moms Talk

I continue to try and make my girls understand that there are several cups I have to fill. Some of those cups are: being there for them and my husband, running my business, and making sure my soul is nourished. So many of the things I do every day are not just for myself. I've had to learn to take time to do things that are meaningful to me and only belong to me.

—Rikki Mor, Knot Genie

I always thought that self-care was something I would do after I got my work done, and then I realized that without taking care of myself, there is no work that gets done. In order for me to feel good and focused, I've got to release my endorphins, stretch my muscles, and clear my brain, body, and soul with exercise and meditation.

—Dr. Elaine Fogel Schneider, Touch Time International

Now we are going to help you identify potential obstacles that can get in the way of your self-care and then list potential solutions to those obstacles. These "obstacles" are really just a mindset, and you can shift that mindset because you are the one who controls your thoughts. We will start the list for you, but please add to it as you see fit.

Potential Obstacle	Potential Rebuttal
I don't have time.	Yes, you do. Look at or rework your schedule.
It's selfish to take time for myself.	People who take good care of themselves are happier and more successful than those who don't.
I don't know what fuels me.	Look at the list of suggestions we shared with you or ask friends for suggestions.
I haven't earned it.	Self-care does not need to be earned. Period.

Drains on Self-Care

Now that you have a better understanding of what you can do to take good care of yourself, let's talk about some things that do just the opposite. The first thing that comes to mind is having so many drains in your life that no amount of self-care will fill you up. By drains, we mean things that sap your energy, things you are putting up with. These can be small: a leaky faucet, a really late thank-you note you need to write, or the fact that winter is approaching and your kids don't have snow boots. Or, they can be big: you have debt that's getting bigger every month, you've been putting off a hard conversation that you need to have with your spouse, or your blood pressure is sky-high and you are paralyzed by the reality of that. We want these issues to be on your radar because they can greatly impact your ability to create the life and business you are planning. (As a side note, if there is some major medical, psychological, or life circumstance that is impacting you, you need to address it. Helping you with that is beyond the scope of this book, but please promise us that you'll get the help you need so you can move forward toward your best possible life.)

Some of these drains are easily handled, while others will require more work. The goal is to take action on the things in life that are dragging you down, because until you do, they will continue to feel like the anchors they are. Tackle the easy ones first and at least begin to make a plan as to how you will manage the others. Until you do, no amount of self-care will be able to offset the effect these drains will have on your life. Write down the things that are holding you back and then come up with the steps you'll need to take to deal with them.

Comparing ourselves to others is another surefire way to undo all of the good of our self-care regimen. Maybe you compare yourself to the neighbor who gets up for her 5 a.m. workouts. Or perhaps you compare yourself to another business owner who was just featured in *Fast Company*. Or maybe you compare yourself to the friend who has time to cook healthy dinners every night. Did we mention that same friend's perfect children eat the healthy dinners with gusto? Not just without complaints—we're talking with real gusto, people. How can you compare? Here's the thing: you can't. And, by the way, there is always more to the story. Perhaps the early morning exerciser goes to bed around 8 p.m., which just wouldn't work for you because that's when you hang out with your husband and you're not about to sacrifice that. Maybe the business owner you admire has a full-time housekeeper and a live-in nanny. And the woman with the kids who eat with gusto? You can bet she has put a lot of time and energy into that healthy cooking at the expense of something else. (We can't explain the non-picky kids; some things can just be chalked up to luck.)

The women you compare yourself to have different life circumstances—for better or for worse—than you do. One woman finds fulfillment through her work. Another finds it by getting in the best shape she's ever been, or in making rolled fondant birthday cakes for her child's third birthday, or in being named PTA volunteer of the year. To each her own. Remember, your life is made up of a series of choices. The point is, none of these choices are wrong. They just might be wrong for *you*. That's what you get to decide. For yourself.

> *Why compare yourself with others? No one in the entire world can do a better job of being you than you.*
> —Unknown

The key here as far as self-care is concerned is that you do the things you want to do and you don't do the things you don't want to do. If having a beautiful garden fills you up, get out there in the dirt. If you feel that you have to have a perfect garden because it's what the neighbors expect from you, it's time to let it go. Remember how saying yes to something means saying no to something else? Keep that in mind.

One of the things we're trying to avoid is becoming a victim or a martyr. One guaranteed way to enter into victim or martyr territory is to do the things you think you *should* do. If there's a book you should read but you don't really want to (parenting books come to mind), read it during some other time than your self-care time. If you *should* meet up with someone you haven't seen in a while but that person zaps your energy when you do hang out, figure out a time to meet her but make sure you don't count it as self-care. If you do, you're likely to end up feeling drained and resentful, which is not what you're going for at all. And be sure to put some boundaries around it, such as only allowing an hour for lunch together and scheduling another appointment after that so you really have to leave.

While we are on the subject, here's how you'll know if something is a good self-care action for you:

1. It's your own idea.
2. It's something you would do more often if you could.
3. It makes you feel really great when you do it.
4. It fills you up and gives you energy to take on the rest of your day.
5. The thought of it makes you just a little bit giddy.
6. It's not folding the laundry.

Again, be careful not to compare your self-care with that of someone else. It doesn't have to look a certain way. The most important thing is to make sure it's something that benefits your wellbeing.

For the Reluctant

This section is for those of you who still can't wrap your head around the fact that self-care is important and, for most of us, necessary. Ponder this: If you think self-care is selfish, just think of it as selling parenthood to your kids by showing your kids that parents still get to have fun and do things that they enjoy. Do you want your kids to learn from your behaviors? Do you want them to learn that they deserve to take good care of themselves, that they should put themselves at the top of their to-do list? We all want our kids to grow up and have healthy, productive, and enjoyable lives. Show them this is possible by modeling it for them. Fill your own tank so you can take care of them.

Moms Talk

I'm the only one to blame when I forget to take great care of myself. In fact, every person in my day-to-day life (my husband, my stepchildren, my friends, my employees, and my clients) encourages me to take time for myself. And I know I'm a better wife, stepmom, and employer when I do. So why is this so hard to remember? In my business, the days fly by, often without me having a chance to think about what I will do for myself. I'm not aiming for perfection and I may always struggle with balancing everything in my life, but I do know when enough is enough. When I hit that point, at least I have the flexibility to take a break or even take a whole day off.

—Traci Bartee, Fly Fitness

One more note from the pulpit: Self-care is not only for the fragile among us. Or the weak. Self-care is something we all need to one degree or another. In fact, in these days of online businesses open 24/7, of Twitter and texting and e-mail and flash sales, and of running kids to one activity or another, it's more important than ever to take some time each day to refuel. Rather than thinking of it as selfish or as just another task, think of it as nurturing your personal well-being, taking a break from the near-constant barrage of information, and setting yourself up for success.

Rewards

Your self-care Hit List can be a great reminder to take care of yourself, but we'd like you to consider building in incentives for your hard work as well. With so many responsibilities, you'll need a few exciting things to look forward to. Some well-deserved rewards, be they lovely things you buy for yourself or simply ways to spend much-needed time off, are often just what you need when you've been busy building a business and taking care of your family.

Let's start with time off. Research shows that taking time off, even if it's just 24 hours, has a profound effect on your mental health. Just imagine what taking a week off could do for you. (And when we say *time off*, we mean *time off*. If you're on a beach somewhere checking e-mail and voice mails, that doesn't count.) We know there can be limitations when it comes to taking time off as an entrepreneur. Time and money are usually the biggest ones, but there are others as well. We'll address those limitations in a minute, but for now, pretend that no limitations exist. If you had the chance to design some time off as a reward for a job well done, what would it be? A big family vacation? A spa getaway with a girlfriend? A week off at home to recharge? Write down the type of time off you'd like to have.

Now, think about what the time away from work would give you. For instance, if you wrote down "a trip by myself," you might say that it would give you some solitude, some time when you are only responsible for yourself, and/or a chance to catch your breath. If you wrote down "a family vacation," that would potentially give you the chance to get away from work, time to reconnect with your family, and/or a brief escape from reality. Go back now and translate your desired time away into the qualities the time off would provide.

It's action time. Ideally, you can now look at your time-off goal(s) and build in a realistic timeframe to give yourself one or more of them. If so, great. Mark the dates on the calendar and relish the time leading up to it. If not, let's home in on what you are craving. To use our earlier example, if you wrote down "a trip by myself," which would give you some much-needed solitude, but the fantasy trip just isn't in the cards right now, think about what *is* possible. What else could you do that would give you some of the solitude you are craving? Could you take just one day away from the house and the family? Could you build some solitude into each of your days for a week? What if your goal was to take a family vacation but it's just not possible? If you are yearning for connection, how about planning a couple of in-house game or movie nights? If you are dying for a shared family experience, maybe you could take a day trip to a nearby town to explore or plan a family hike. The idea here is to reward yourself with whatever it is that you are yearning for. It doesn't have to be extravagant—although, if time and money allow, we are all for a bit of extravagance.

While we're on the subject of rewards, sometimes there is value in setting your sights on something material. Do you loathe your current couch? Are you craving new bedding? Or is there a winter jacket you've been eyeing but just can't justify? How about linking that reward to a business milestone that you can work toward? For instance, *If I get five new clients, I'll buy myself that coat.* Experts are divided on whether or not it's healthy to reward children with material goods for a job well done, but the experts don't get to decide what's right for you as a mom business owner. If you know you'll be motivated by a new piece of furniture, by all means let yourself work toward a business goal that will end in a personal victory as well. Take a few minutes now to write down a few rewards that you would ultimately like to give yourself and then link them to a business goal that makes sense.

Rewards can come in a lot of different shapes and sizes. When it's not the right time for a major reward (family vacation or home renovation, for instance), it's still possible to reward yourself with something. On the next page are some great ideas to get you started.

Self-Talk

We all have an internal voice that seems to chat almost nonstop from the time we wake up until the time we fall asleep. That chatter in and of itself is not the issue. It's when the chatter is negative, nagging, and downright rude that the problem arises. Have you ever taken the time to listen to some of the things you say to yourself? It can be enlightening to spend a few minutes noticing, because that voice is not always kind.

And what about the stories we tell ourselves? We create stories that hold us back (*I'm not a writer*, *Nobody will believe me*, or *Who am I to expect a high level of success?*), and we tell stories that are really excuses ("People like me don't do that sort of thing," or "I could do it if only I were younger"). Who makes this stuff up? We do, and we need to notice when we are doing it so we can stop ourselves when it happens.

Reward Yourself

Free

- listen to some of your favorite songs, or one favorite song over and over
- go for a walk
- call a friend for a nice, long chat
- take a nice, long hot bath
- catch up with your DVR
- go on a bike ride
- take a day off--completely off--from work

$

- treat yourself to a cappuccino and sit in the coffee shop to savor it
- go see a movie
- buy yourself some really decadent chocolate
- buy yourself some flowers
- get a favorite magazine and let yourself read it all in one sitting
- take yourself out to lunch
- go see an art exhibit
- get new nail polish or lip gloss

$$

- schedule dinner out at a restaurant you've been wanting to try
- take a day trip to a nearby town
- buy yourself a new outfit
- have a manicure or a pedicure (or both)
- hire someone to clean your house (even if it's just once)
- buy tickets to a performance you've been wanting to see

$$$

- take a vacation
- buy something you've been wanting for your home
- have a spa day
- invest in a hobby: buy a guitar and lessons, get some art supplies you've been wanting, etc.

Moms Talk

Sometimes I find myself weaving a story about how others are somehow more capable and brilliant and braver than I am, and it immediately takes me to a desperate place. I know this place—it's where I feel a strong sense of urgency and my breathing gets shallow. It has to happen now, or else everything will fall apart. I know now that this is my ego, and that feeding it by buying into the negative self-talk only makes it grow bigger. When I step back, I can actually find the humor in it—in the extravagance of my worst-case-scenario-ing or how-awful-I-must-really-be-ness. In reality, it is a moment, and the moment will pass, and I will still be standing here perfectly capable of handling what shows up. And so that is what I remind myself when my ego wants to hijack the moment.

—Erin Dullea, 52 Dares

We all have that little voice inside who is intent on putting us down. I call mine my "inner bully." Our inner bully wants to stop us in our tracks. And it will if we let it. The inner bully compares and wants you to focus on your "shortcomings." To defeat it, choose to celebrate your uniqueness and that of those around you. Remind yourself that your journey is not right or wrong; it is simply yours. The inner bully also competes. Society and culture want us to be "super moms" or "top executives," but you know what? It's not a race, it's a journey, and we have to collaborate with each other to achieve our desired results.

—Elayna Fernandez, The Positive Mom

Overcoming negative self-talk requires discipline, just like breaking any other bad habit. In every moment, we choose our thoughts, and unfortunately most of our default thoughts are not in our best interests and can sabotage our efforts. It's important to be mindful moment to moment of what you're thinking so you can recognize a negative thought as it appears and consciously replace it with a more empowering thought. Doing this will change your life.

—Debra Gano, BYOU (Be Your Own You) Magazine

Before every session, I wonder if I have it in me to take images that are going to make this specific client happy. It doesn't matter that I've done successful sessions over and over; I still question myself before every one. To help stop the negativity, I look through past session images on my phone, and find myself really liking what I see. By doing that, I am reminded that I know how to do this and soon the negative voice is replaced by something more like, "I have got this!"

—Margie Scherschligt, Margie Photo

This is also a good place to watch for rules that you've made up for yourself: *I can't _____ because _____*. It's funny how we'll set up a rule for ourselves and then diligently follow that rule even if it makes no sense. "I can't watch a show on my DVR during the day because that would make me lazy," said by the woman who spends all of her evenings answering work-related e-mails. "I can't take a day off because there wouldn't be anyone to answer customers' questions," says another. (This one is easily fixed by setting up an auto reply stating that you are away from the office for the day and will get back to them tomorrow.) You get the idea. Be aware of those types of rules and be ready to question them when you notice them.

If you find that your self-talk could use some cleaning up, here are some ways to handle it.

- ✎ Notice the tone and words of your inner voice.
- ✎ Make an effort to stop the chatter when it turns negative.
- ✎ Consciously replace the negative talk with something more encouraging. Elite athletes are known for using positive affirmations to help them achieve greatness.
- ✎ Practice, practice, practice.

Take a few minutes now to think about some of the things you say to yourself, some of the stories you've made up, and some of the rules you've set up for yourself. Write them down and begin to notice when you hear yourself saying them.

Awareness is the first step toward stopping the negative self-talk. Revealing these negative thoughts for what they are takes away some of their power. It's going to take some practice on your part, but once you start noticing them on a regular basis, you'll be able to replace them with rules and beliefs that empower you.

Erin used to tell herself that she wasn't good at public speaking. She told herself that again and again for years and ended up believing it was true. At some point, though, she started being presented with speaking opportunities. Her first thought was to say no, of course. But something made her stop for a second to look at the opportunity from a more objective place. Once she questioned this rule that she wasn't a good speaker, she had a chance to ask herself if that rule made any sense. She challenged herself and this rule by saying yes to the opportunity to speak to a group of new moms. She didn't have the time of her life but she did survive the experience and she even got a new client out of it. *Take that, negative self-talk.* Now, when she hears that inner voice of hers spouting off about how she's not a good public speaker, she replaces that dialogue with something more along the lines of, *I've done it and I can do it again.* (She doesn't want to lie to herself by saying that she's great at it but she also wants to get out of her own way.)

All of this may seem sort of silly, but our clients have let us in on some of the things they say to themselves, and the words they use are not only unproductive, they are downright offensive at times. It's worth paying attention to it so you can liberate yourself from this nastiness. We are so hard on ourselves. Just think what that constant criticism does to our well-being.

Before we finish up on self-care, we want to mention something that sociologists are calling "contaminated time." According to *Real Simple Magazine*, this term is now being used to describe leisure time that is cluttered up with less enjoyable tasks such as household chores or child care.[1] This is time that we are counting as downtime but that doesn't actually refresh us the way downtime is meant to. Moms are especially susceptible to this so-called contaminated time because a disproportionate amount of house- and child-related responsibility falls on our shoulders. We are not saying that you can't count time with your kids as self-care (remember, we are all about the twofers), but make sure that you are doing something that is truly replenishing. (Think hiking with your daughter or going to a fun museum with your son.)

To stretch you even further, we also want to encourage you to pat yourself on the back when you have done good work. It's great to get outside accolades, and social media is a good place to toot your own horn every once in a while to get some much-needed acknowledgment. But just remember, it's more than okay to tell *yourself* that you did a great job. If you're feeling especially complimentary, you can even send yourself a card congratulating yourself or take yourself out for your favorite beverage. Self-care through the mail and through espresso or wine is great self-care. Cheers to you!

Moms Talk

There comes a moment when our self-talk has become so negative that we seem to blame everything on ourselves and our "imperfection." Being imperfect is what enables us to grow. I grew up in a perfectionist household and I never felt I was good enough, so I decided to break that cycle and commend myself, instead. Remember your achievements, your positive qualities, what the people who love you think of you, and own it!

—Elayna Fernandez, The Positive Mom

Bottom Line

- ✎ Self-care is not a luxury; it's a necessity.
- ✎ There are compelling benefits to be gained by taking great care of yourself.
- ✎ You do not need to earn the right to self-care, and it's not at all selfish to build time for it into your schedule.
- ✎ Planning out and scheduling your self-care ensures that you will have time for it, even on the busiest of days.
- ✎ Taking time away from work and also managing your self-talk are important components of any self-care plan.

Part II

Own Your Business

Chapter 5

Your Toolkit

As a mom entrepreneur, you have many resources available to you (some you may not even realize you have) that can help you in your business. We call these resources your toolkit. This chapter focuses on helping you identify those resources so you can put them to work for you. These resources include strengths, skills, personality traits, education, and past work and volunteer experience, as well as your human resources, your connections, and your support system. It's likely you know how to use at least some of these to your advantage as a business owner. Perhaps just as important, it's likely there are tools in your kit that you don't currently use that could prove to be very helpful.

Even if you have been in business for a while, it's well worth taking the time to reassess the items in your tool-kit from time to time. We've established that being both a mom and a business owner comes with its own set of challenges (is that the understatement of the year?), so the goal here is to use all the resources you have to make things as easy as possible on yourself. To ensure that you leave no stone unturned, it's important to articulate your resources and write them down. By making use of everything that is available to you, you can more easily build a business that doesn't require you to stretch yourself thin at every step. Now let's get you on track to owning all of those assets and determining what you can do to make them work for you and your business.

Strengths

Let's start by jotting down your strengths.

What do you do better than most people? What do other people always tell you you're good at? Strengths can be surprisingly hard to come up with because you might just take them for granted. They are so easy for you that you just assume everyone can do them. Think back to your childhood, your time in school, and other work experiences you've had. Your parents, teachers, and past bosses all likely let you know what they saw as your strengths. In addition, think of the things that just come naturally to you. Are you great at connecting people? Do you have a flair for helping others understand complicated ideas? Are you naturally organized? Do people constantly tell you that you give the most creative gifts? Take some time to think about the things you can claim as your strengths and then write them down. Be sure not to edit yourself. You may think of something you're good at but discount its importance because it doesn't seem to relate to your business. Write it down anyway. There's a chance you won't be able to use it to your advantage, but you might, so make sure it's on your list.

If you're having a hard time coming up with your strengths, we highly recommend Tom Rath's *Strengthsfinder 2.0*.[1] The book comes with a code that allows you to take the well-known Strengthsfinder assessment online. Completing the assessment will go a long way toward helping you know and understand what you are good at. For instance, it could help you discover that your love of learning is a strength. Or maybe it will uncover your strength of researching information. The assessment might also help you realize that despite being told all your life you talk too much, one of your top strengths is being a powerful communicator—a highly valued skill in today's workplace. Whether you call them strengths, gifts, or talents, these are the unique elements that make you who you are. And, as Rath points out in *Strengthsfinder 2.0*, you'll go much further in life by playing to your strengths than by trying to compensate for your weaknesses. As an entrepreneur, playing to your strengths will definitely save you time and money as well as help propel you toward your goals.

Once you've made your list, be sure to ask close friends and family members what they see as your strengths. It can make you feel vulnerable to ask a question like this so feel free to tell people we are making you do it—we're happy to take the blame on this one. If it's more comfortable for you, send the request via e-mail. That way, nobody is put on the spot, and the recipients have some time to gather their thoughts before responding to you. A simple e-mail like this will do the trick: "Hi. I'm doing a self-assessment for which I need to gather opinions from the people who know me best. What would you say are my top three strengths?" Be sure to add to your list based on the responses you get.

Skills

Skills are the things you see listed in a Help Wanted ad or on your own resume. It's possible you listed some skills as strengths. That's fine; there is often some overlap. But for skills, think about more specific, task-based actions such as Website design, copy writing, or bookkeeping. Skills are those things that you can do that not everyone can do. Again, this isn't the time to limit yourself. If you spent a few years in college teaching dance lessons but you can't imagine how that will help you in your current business, write it down anyway. This is meant to be as exhaustive an inventory of your skills as possible, so include any and all that you can think of. Maybe you studied Spanish for years and can pass for fluent. Chances are your skills will include things like running a fundraiser, managing a budget, or public speaking. When compiling this list, think about past education, past jobs, past volunteer experiences, hobbies, and even some of the skills you've acquired as a mom. Pretty much every mom we know has acquired some mean project-management and logistics skills throughout the years. Write down whatever comes to mind, and leave space because you just might think of more things as we go along.

Personality Traits

Let's move on to some personality traits that can be valuable to mom entrepreneurs. We have spoken to hundreds of mom business owners throughout the years, and these same traits have come up again and again: grit, courage, confidence, and patience. Of course, these aren't the only worthwhile traits to have as a mom business owner, but these, along with passion (which we covered in Chapter 1) and vision (which we covered in Chapter 2), are the ones that really seem to stand out.

Now, some of these traits may come naturally to you, and others...well, not so much. That's okay. We are pointing them out so that you can give yourself credit for them in your toolkit and put them to work if you have them. They can all be learned and/or strengthened if you choose, so please don't despair if you look through the list and feel as though none of them are words you would necessarily associate strongly with yourself. Let's dive a little deeper and explore these personality traits a bit, shall we?

Grit

Grit is defined as perseverance and passion for long-term goals. We think of it as the willingness to stick with something no matter what. It's the ability to keep going even after you've run into obstacle after obstacle. Grit is a strong internal force that drives people toward their goals. This characteristic is one that researchers are now paying a lot of attention to because studies have shown that people with grit tend to have more success than those without it. One of the main researchers studying grit, Angela Duckworth from the University of Pennsylvania, says, "The gritty individual approaches achievement as a marathon; his or her advantage is stamina."[2] Did we mention that owning a business—especially as a mom—is a marathon and not a sprint? Grit comes in really handy when you're working on something long-term.

Think about the people you know who seem to have a lot of grit. You may have noticed them because they are so committed to their goals and aspirations that they don't let anything else get in their way. Sure, they have their challenges. Life turns upside-down for them at times, just as it does for all of us. But the gritty among us don't let obstacles derail them. Instead, they adjust their path. They overcome complications. They move mountains if they have to, and they stay the course. And because of their level of commitment, life works out well for them. Some call it luck; others know that what they are seeing is actually grit.

Studies have shown that people who have grit have greater success in a variety of pursuits. The principle is one that even the smallest child can understand: how many times have you given in to your kids just because they weren't willing to stop asking? It's a similar situation when you are looking for sales for your company's product or service: deciding to take every no as a "maybe later" seems to be one way to secure future business.

It's not just about being persistent with your customers. It's about having the ability to fail, dust yourself off, and try again because you just know that what you are doing is worth it. The most successful people in work and in life understand that the best learning is in the mistakes, and that not every effort proves fruitful. Those who keep going no matter what are rewarded. It's as simple as that.

> *It's not that I'm so smart, it's just that I stay with problems longer.*
> —Albert Einstein

Grit isn't something you need to call on all day every day. It's almost as though it's simmering in the background so you can access it when you need it. And we don't all have it in equal measure. Those who have easy access to grit can usually go the extra mile, whereas those who haven't yet learned how to summon it might choose to get in bed and pull the covers over their heads. But this is not a place for despair; you can have less grit and still find success. You just might want to put into place the support you need to keep at it, such as hiring a coach or finding an accountability partner, because the journey you are on will call for grit, and it's worth your time if you can build that muscle.

Moms Talk

"Fake it 'til you make it" is a tired business cliché, but one I have lived profitably since I started my business in 2006. When I left the safety of a New York branding agency, I needed to offer something different in order to compete. I came up with the idea of talking to real people in the real world to find out what they really think and capturing it on video—kind of reality TV meets market research.

To sell the idea, I needed a demo tape. I had no money to pay a professional, and I'm a technology idiot, but that didn't stop me. On a bitter February morning in Chicago, I stood outside the original Marshall Field's department store to ask shoppers how they felt about it becoming Macy's. The rumble of elevated trains drowned out peoples' answers and I ended up with lots of footage of peoples' feet. As hard as shooting was, editing was worse. I had no idea how to use the software. Turning raw footage into a compelling story structure was a real challenge. The result was truly a mess. Undaunted, I loaded that mess onto YouTube and sent press releases everywhere. Shock of shocks, I got a call from the ABC affiliate in Chicago asking to interview me and cover my story on air. Years later, video market research is a mainstay of my company's service offerings and I have worked for some of the world's best-known brands. The school of hard knocks is easy to get into, but it takes real moxie to earn a degree.

—Lisa Merriam, Merriam Associates

Many days I have to wake up and say to myself what my Grandma once said: "Get behind yourself and PUSH!" I'm pretty sure I still don't know what I am doing, more often than not, but I get behind myself and PUSH. When I hit a low spot, I have a rule: I say to myself, "Susan, you get 24 hours to boo-hoo all you want, and then it's go time. PUSH!" I don't know if the day will ever come that I don't have to tell myself that, but for now, I am hitting success in the bull's eye.

—Susan Slater Cotter, Strength Studio

Throughout the years Startup Princess has grown and shifted. Similar to many companies, we've had pivot points in our business that have helped us change directions to meet the needs of small business owners all across the world. Also similar to many companies, we've hit snags along the way and have made our fair share of mistakes. In the fall of 2013 our site was hit by hackers and was down for about six weeks. We'd get it fixed and then it would get hit again. We tried lots of tech specialists, worked with our host, installed

"Site Doctor," and so much more. I remember asking myself, "Is this a sign? Are we supposed to take this site down?" And then I remembered some of my own words ringing in my ears: "This is not a sign, it is a trial of your fate."

A long time ago I stopped looking at failures or setbacks as the world telling me I'm headed in the wrong direction. I now see them as the world saying to me, "Are you going to make excuses or Make It Happen?" Trial comes to test our conviction and make us stronger. Business isn't about things always running smoothly; in fact, it's a bumpy ride. But every experience prepares us for the next and every experience gives us important opportunities to grow and come out on top.

—Michelle McCullough, Startup Princess

You can easily see that a non-negotiable inner commitment pays off. You, as a mom entrepreneur, are going to face many conflicting priorities and challenges daily, and you don't have the luxury of waiting for things to be convenient or easy. That's why dedication to your dream and perseverance is so critical. The women whose stories you just read put a stake in the ground, and from then on, everything they did came from that one decision. The stake created the path for them to move toward their goals without anything (at least not anything permanent) getting in their way.

Here is the glaring, undeniable truth: sometimes it would be easier to just throw in the towel. Managing the responsibilities that go with being a mother and a business owner could overwhelm even the most steadfast among us. But grit, that unwillingness or even inability to give up, can be a big asset. Some might call it stubbornness; what we know about it, though, is that even if every day can't be a total success, keeping at something that you truly want to do and that reflects who you are will lead to great things.

Confidence

Many of us have been held back by the belief that we don't have what it takes or what others are looking for. From our experience working with women, we can't begin to count the number of times our clients have downplayed their experience or assumed that what they had done was not enough to result in all that they wanted out of life. But when you look at real-life examples of successful people, you'll notice they will often say that it was a stroke of luck that got them where they are. Or it was hard work and blissful ignorance of how much they didn't know. Much of what successful people do has to do with believing in themselves and having the ability to make others believe in them too, even if that doesn't happen right away. Unwavering confidence and knowing you can get the job done even if you fail along the way? Seems like a winning combination to us.

A sense of self-worth or confidence is largely tied up in knowing that you can fail without being a failure. If you feel as though you are enough just as you are, then you will have the confidence to go out into the world, be told *no*, and not take it personally; you'll have the confidence to fall down and get back up; you'll have the ability to make a wrong choice and then choose differently the next time. Often, that's the difference between someone who keeps going and someone who gives up. Those who lack confidence lack the willingness to take the next logical step in life and in business, and if you don't move forward, guess what? Not much happens to get you where you want to go.

What if you are lacking in the confidence department? Is there a way to build it? Of course there is, and it's easier than you may think. One of the best ways to build your confidence is to fail. That's right, ladies, we are encouraging you to fail. It's not the failing that builds confidence, though; it's what happens afterward. When you dust yourself off and get back up so you can keep going, you've just increased your confidence (and your grit). Voilà!

Another great way to build your confidence is to do something that makes you feel a sense of success. It doesn't even have to be related to work. Run a 5K, make a soufflé, or finally spend an hour or two putting together a photo album (you know it's on your *someday* list). Getting a bit of success under your belt is a fabulous way to build up your confidence (and if you get to eat soufflé as a result, then so much the better).

Ridding your life of comparisons is another way to bolster your confidence. We mentioned this earlier but it's worth repeating: when you are constantly measuring your self-worth by what others have accomplished, it's a losing battle. Instead, how about setting some benchmarks for yourself and then taking action on them? Measuring yourself today compared to where you were a year ago is a much more constructive and accurate way to see what progress you've made. And measuring where you are today against where you eventually want to be can give you the motivation to keep going. This is why creating and working according to a business plan is so helpful. You get to set powerful goals for yourself and then see your progress. We'll dig into that in Chapter 6.

Moms Talk

To bolster my confidence in business, I have created a motto: "Never assume no." As I've used the motto over time, it has helped build my confidence from within. And it really works. For example, when I had the idea for "StinkyKids: The Musical," based on my books, I told myself, "Never assume no," which helped me get up the nerve to call Vital Theater Company in New York, thinking they would be a good fit. Two weeks later we were in the beginning stages of production.

—Britt Menzies, StinkyKids

Courage

Someone has to be the first at everything, and it's usually those people who know they don't know how to do something but forge ahead regardless, flexing their courage muscle along the way. Of the many women we spoke to when working on this book, a clear theme was that they didn't know what they were getting into and that the not knowing was actually an asset in many ways. Did they give up when they didn't know? Did they retreat to a safe place? No, they admitted they didn't know. They sought out and asked questions of those who might know. And they moved ahead, making mistakes along the way, until they were solidly in the camp of knowing. (Have you noticed a theme here around making mistakes, failing, and then getting back up again?)

That's how learning works. First, though, you have to admit you don't know, and that's a scary place for many people. Admitting that usually leads us to seek a safe haven, which almost always means retreat. And that's the opposite of what a successful business person does. It takes a certain amount of courage to start something new. If that something new is a business and you plan to start or grow the business while also being a mom, it takes a monumental amount of courage. The English word *courage* comes from the French word *courage*, which means heart. So when you muster up the courage to move forward toward a goal or outcome that you want to accomplish, you are actually moving toward it with your heart, and that can be a vulnerable place. The women we spoke with had a lot of heart, and although we readily admit that it takes more than just heart to succeed as an entrepreneur, if you're willing to lean into the experience and be courageous, you'll be off to a great start.

Many women we spoke with about their journey as entrepreneurs found more courage along the way than they thought they had. It's funny how once you decide to pursue something important, you aren't willing to let not knowing or the threat of looking stupid stop you. And guess what? If you don't let it stop you, often others won't stop you either. Believe it or not, our dumb mistakes are often just the thing that makes others like us. Those mistakes make us human. Plus, not knowing sometimes allows you to break some of the unwritten rules that, if followed, just might slow you down or get in your way. And one more thing: often, when you turn up the volume on your courage, the volume of your negative self-talk turns down on its own. Try it. You just may love the results.

Courage, as with the rest of these traits, is something you can build. It's going to take getting comfortable with being uncomfortable, though. You'll need to take risks. You'll need to not know and be okay with that. Rather than feeling fearful in a new situation, try to focus on the fact that you are about to learn something. It always helps to focus on the intention and the desired outcome, which, in this case, is moving you closer to your vision for your life.

Just for fun, think of some small things you could do to increase your level of courage. You'll know you are on the right track when you feel butterflies in your stomach or think to yourself with a tiny grin, *Could I actually do that?* Write down two or three things that you've been thinking of doing but that also scare the bejeepers out of you.

Moms Talk

I have to give one piece of advice: if you decide to [open a business], you have to know going in that it will be the scariest thing you've ever done. There will be moments of real fear, and you have to be absolutely willing to stare down that fear regularly. It gets easier at times, but it's not going to be easy. And you just have to know that, and know that there are great days and really hard days, and it's scary most of the time. It takes courage. It's the courage to go against the voices in your head, your mother's voice, your friends' voices, and the voices telling you "You can't do it." It's really just having the courage to keep going.

—Sharelle Klaus, Dry Soda

I couldn't find a job so I had to create a job. My advice? Go in feet first and be a little naive.

—Naomi Lewis, High Maintenance Skincare Studio

My willingness to not know but do it anyway helped me get started. Overall, I like this quality about myself because it allows me to take risks. If I had listened to everyone's opinions, or spent years learning all about business process, I might have become reluctant and decided not to do it. For the most part, I usually get a hunch about something, mull it around in my head for a while, and then just do it.

—Cathy Tousley, Furlesse

I didn't allow myself to get caught up in "what if" questions. You could easily get frozen by what you don't have ready or what you don't yet know, but if you're confident in your product or service, that's all you need.

—Cause Haun, See Kai Run

Patience

In this fast-paced world of ours, patience seems to be a dying trait. We want what we want and we want it *now*. (Does that sound familiar? Are you now suddenly and inexplicably thinking of your children?) However, successful business owners know the value of delayed gratification and have learned firsthand the lessons of that old adage, "Good things come to those who wait." There is a real art to knowing when to push through full-throttle and when to note that the timing might not be quite right in that moment. Most mom entrepreneurs wish they could do it all at once, but many realize that by having patience and allowing things to unfold naturally, they are readying themselves for future success.

As we mentioned before, growing a business is much more of a marathon than a sprint. Those who are used to near-instant success will find that the process may take much longer than they would like. Building your business is like being pregnant: there is that initial rush of excitement followed by months of changes that show gradually. (We'll expand on this analogy in the next chapter.) The average new business doesn't make a profit for three to five years, so, although you may dream of instant success, and we can always hold out hope for that, it's a good idea to have a hefty supply of patience in your back pocket just in case you need it.

Some people may confuse being patient with just sitting back and passively waiting for things to come their way, but patience is really more about action. Those who are patient don't expect instant results, so while they are waiting for what they want they are also actively pursuing things that will bring their goals into reality. Patience isn't a license to kick back and eat bonbons (what *is* a bonbon, anyway?). Patience means gracefully and continually pursuing things that will get you where you want to be.

Patience is a virtue, and it's one that not many of us have in excess. In today's fast-paced world, it is almost a lost art. We believe that patience and persistence are like yin and yang: one requires and completes the other. Our contributors were able to point toward this fact: if you can be patient while still working toward your goals, that ability will likely pay off. Plus, just think about the benefits to you and your family if that patience muscle of yours gets stronger. We picture your loved ones not having to endure that frantic "hurry up and get your shoes on" hollering as often, and maybe that huge client you've been carefully and persistently following up with for months finally telling you he's ready to sign on the dotted line.

We're not suggesting you have no control over when and how things happen; as an entrepreneur and a mom, you'll have plenty to keep you busy. Waiting for success also gives you time to get still during those impatient moments and listen to your inner voice for guidance. It also gives you a chance to practice for when you hit the big time.

Moms Talk

I knew I had a good idea and, initially, I envisioned people flocking to my Website and that I would appear on Oprah almost immediately. It would all be so easy; a great product would definitely equal instant success. I didn't give much thought to all the steps in between: a realistic timeline, manufacturing, developing marketing materials, creating a Website, or even drawing up a sales and distribution strategy. And what happens after the product launch? I knew that I would have to face those issues eventually, but in the beginning, I didn't want reality to get in the way of making my dream come true. I would figure it out; I always had. I prided myself in being a creative problem-solver and I knew the road to success would be a series of solving problems one at a time.

—Veronica Mayo, Vemayca

In January of 2013, I launched Make It Happen Radio as an extension of my platform and to aid in the promotion of my speaking business. At the time, we had about 200,000 followers on Twitter, a loyal fan base, and powerful Web traffic. I expected the show to pick up right away with tens of thousands of downloads and listeners a month. As you can guess, it was slow growing at first. I had measly downloads in the hundreds for the first few months and almost threw in the towel. Sometimes we expect things to happen overnight in business. We want our product or service to be an overnight sensation. But all good things take time to grow and adapt. Marketing is a ripple effect. Some people have to catch on and help it spread. Don't throw in the towel for any promotional model right away. Be patient. Give it time to turn heads and then you'll watch the ripple effect grow.

—Michelle McCullough, Startup Princess

Patience and persistence pay off every day for me. One of my faves? When I published my book, *Found It,* I e-mailed The UPS Store with a request to sell my book in all their stores around the country because I mention them as a resource. Bold? Yes. Silly? Maybe. They finally replied and said, "Thanks but no thanks." So I continued to persistently e-mail and e-mail again, requesting it, and pointing out why they should, and I continued to be told no. Finally, and fortunately, a reader tweeted that she loved my book and had no idea that The UPS Store offered mailboxes but thanks to my book she now knew. I retweeted that, cc'd the company, and basically said, "SEE???" Although they continued to say no to my original request, they did finally agree to promote any type of video I made featuring the book and The UPS Store. That is how I ended up making a commercial for them, posting it to YouTube, and having them promote it via their Website, newsletter, and social media. It ended up being great promo for me and I still get to talk about that video.

—Jill Salzman, Founding Moms

Now that we've explored the personality traits in your personal toolkit, let's move on and explore another area that is usually full of tools you can leverage in your business.

Work and Volunteer Experience

Education, jobs, and volunteer experiences are other places to look for things that can be included in your toolkit. Some of the items here may overlap with strengths or skills, but it's still important to mine these areas for valuable resources. For instance, if you studied marketing in college, you may not consider it a strength or a skill, but you know more than someone who didn't study it. If you volunteered at a women's shelter, that experience may not seem to connect directly with selling whatever fabulous product your business specializes in, but something you learned during that experience just might come in handy.

Take some time to go back through your experiences and add to your list for your toolkit. Maybe you used to schedule someone else's meetings and you got pretty good at it. Perhaps you started out working on spreadsheets in Excel and, though you haven't done it in a while, you might still remember a thing or two. For example, one of our clients was an attorney in her former life. Although she was excited to leave that career behind when she opened her preschool enrichment programs, her experience in reading complex legal documents and in negotiating led to her successfully orchestrating franchise deals for her company. Go ahead and jog your memory by pulling out a copy of your resume. You just might come across something you had completely forgotten about.

While we are on the subject of past experiences, it's also a good idea to think about negative experiences you've had and what you learned from them. For instance, Erin had several jobs between college and Magnolia Workshop. All of them were in marketing or advertising and in all of them she had a boss. Common enough, but here's the thing: She never really thrived while she was working for someone else. She did fine; she got through the days and did a good job. But it wasn't until after she had kids and began working for herself that she realized how much she truly flourished with the independence, flexibility, and autonomy she now had. We never like to say *never*, but there is a pretty good chance that Erin will not go to work for someone else again. *With* someone? That's a real possibility. *For* someone? Probably not. Although what we just described isn't really a tool, it is valuable information for Erin to have as she moves forward in her career. Think about some of your seemingly negative experiences and write down any lessons you can glean from them.

Your Human Resources

Although "knowing people" isn't a tool in the same sense as the other things we've talked about, who you know can be pivotal in moving your business in the direction you want it to go. You know the saying: "It's all who you know." Well, we wouldn't say it's *everything*, not even close, but it really can lead to shortcuts and faster growth. Take some time to think about your business and about the people in your life who could potentially help you in some way.

Related to that, every mom we interviewed had created a strong support system. For some, that was their husband and children. For others, it included friends, extended family, and mentors. Because of the world of social networking, some of the women we spoke with said that their most ardent supporters were women they had never even met in person. Thanks to sites such as Twitter and Facebook, the support available to mom entrepreneurs is seemingly endless. We feel lucky to be named among our clients' greatest supporters, many of whom we've never met in person. (Did we mention that even though we wrote a book together, we hadn't met face to face until it was written? We were happy to discover that neither of us was some old man sitting in his basement...it would have just been weird, you know?) No matter what your support system looks like, know this: most of us would not get by without one. If you're just starting out on this journey as a mom entrepreneur and you don't yet have a strong network of supporters, building one should really be your first order of business. It's that important.

The role of your support network will vary from day to day. Some days you might need a friend to listen to you complain. Other days, a family member may be called upon to pick up your child from school. Your husband may be your sounding board for new business ideas. Your coach or mentor can be the one you rely on when it comes to making pivotal decisions for your company. And your kids can help you package up products for shipping or be responsible for getting dinner on the table. (Who doesn't love cereal and toast for dinner?) Having a wide network of people on whom you can rely can make the stresses of starting and running your own business much easier to handle.

Moms Talk

I try every day to make my kids a part of the business. It might be my math-whiz son adding up numbers for me and giving projections, or my daughter giving her input on a design. I also take them to my office with me after school, where they run around in the warehouse and play games behind the racks. They understand what it takes to start a business and know how much time you have to put into it. So if I miss a field trip permission slip, or forget about a birthday party I was supposed to take them to, we all just have a big laugh about it as I admit to them what a lame parent I can be at times.

—Hilary Genga, Trunkettes

This seems like a good time to point out something that may be obvious: Your support system is not there to always tend to your needs. It's likely that these same people will need *your* help from time to time. In fact, in our humble opinions, it's the reciprocity factor of these relationships that makes them work so well. So think about how you can lend your support and help to others. We'll give you a chance to cultivate and grow your support network later in this chapter. For now, here are some examples of just how crucial your friends and family can be.

Moms Talk

We spent a lot of time talking to women who had started their own businesses. We'd have them over for coffee or a glass of wine and kind of pick their brains and get some good ideas that way. Have a good network of people that you then can call on if you have a question—which you'll have a bunch of.

—Karen Whorton, ReUsies

Social media sites like Facebook, Twitter, Pinterest, and YouTube really level the playing field between the big companies and smaller ones, so take advantage of them! Using them is invaluable and usually free. Network, network, network— whether it's with your target customers or with experts who can fill gaps in your skill set.

—Julie Cole, Mabel's Labels and parenting blogger

In the last few years, I have started to learn how to build a strong support system and a hard-working team of people on whom I can call to help me. Creating this network has been the smartest thing I have done in business. It took many years of working constantly to learn that one. I have always struggled with delegating tasks; I intrinsically think that I have to do everything. Plus, I am a certifiable control freak. It has been a challenge to allow others to help me with the various tasks of working on projects and running a business, but it has also been worth it.

—Sue Anne Morgan, IdeaLand

In the beginning I felt like I needed to sell my bags to wholesalers. There was huge opportunity by going down that path, but because my manufacturing was here in Seattle, my margins weren't ideal for wholesaling. Luckily, I had a community of mom business owners who shared their stories of what business models were working for them. One woman in particular focused only on direct sales from her Website. That really made sense to me and made me realize that I don't have to wholesale and that my business doesn't have to look a certain way or follow a certain path. It's like the Wild West in business right now, and the part I enjoy most is that I get to decide what is best for my business. Because of this, I can put my time and energy where it is most necessary rather than spreading myself thin doing what I think I'm "supposed to" do.

—Sarah Kirk, Swoop Bags

We just can't do it alone. No matter how independent you are, we can guarantee that you will need some help along the way. Having a strong support system lets you handle the unexpected and lifts you up when you need it. Numerous studies have shown the benefits of having a strong network that you can count on. According to studies cited in an article by the Mayo Clinic, those benefits include: a sense of belonging, an increased sense of self-worth, the feeling of security, and a greater ability to combat stress.[3] All of these benefits will greatly improve your chances of success in both business and life.

If you want a strong support system, you have to build it. And, as is often the case with creating something that involves other people, you will likely get out of it what you put into it. So, let's get to work. Grab a pen and paper and draw two columns on the paper. In the left column, list a person (or just list the role if you don't yet know whom you'd call on for this support). In the right column across from each person/role you list, consider what support you can count on them to provide.

Here's an example to get you started.

Person/Role	Support They Can Provide
Partner/spouse	Childcare, household help, errands, brainstorming
Older children	Household, dinner, laundry, packaging, data entry, childcare
Neighbor	Help with packaging during busy season
Friend	Pick up your child from school in a pinch, act as a cheerleader when you need someone to encourage you

Putting Your Toolkit to Work

There are several reasons we're asking you to articulate the tools in your toolkit.

One: We want to jog your memory for any hidden assets you may be able to call on down the road.

Two: This is a confidence-builder. Once you take a look at a written list of all of the things you can do, you'll likely start feeling pretty darned proud and competent.

Three: When you play to your strengths, things go much more smoothly. Think about how much easier it is for an adult to cut up her food than it is for a kid. Using a knife and fork is new to a child. It's a weakness. But for the adult who has been doing it for years, it's probably a strength; not one you want to hang your hat on, but it's a strength nonetheless. Now, think about the frustration that often comes the first several (hundred) times kids try to cut their food. Think of the ease with which you do it. Which one seems more appealing? This leads us to the last purpose.

Four: When you are doing things that come easily to you or that you've had practice doing, you don't have to spend much energy doing them. That unused energy can then be used elsewhere.

There is one thing we want to mention again here because we know at least some of you will go to this place: If you find that your strengths, skills, personality traits, experience, and community don't look as good on paper as you would hope, please don't despair. This is not meant to make you feel bad about what you don't have. After all, many factors go into building and managing a successful business, and many people have found great success without the "right" education, without much past experience in the working world, and without having what they deem to be enough connections. If you find your list lacking in some way, please don't use it to limit yourself or what's possible for you. We know you've gained some great skills and experience in the last few decades, and this is your chance to shine a light on them and put them to good use.

Strengths and Skills Inventory

Grab your pen and divide a piece of paper into three columns as you see in the following example. In the left column, list first your strengths and then your skills. In the second column, write "yes" or "no" to say whether you're leveraging those strengths or skills in your work now. In the last column, note whether you would like to use each strength or skill more or less in your work. Here's an example for you.

Strengths/Skills	Do I leverage it in my work now? (Yes/No)	Do I want to use this more in my work? (+/-)
Leadership	No	+
Writing	Yes	+

Organizing	Yes	-
Researching	Yes	+

Now, take a look at your Strengths and Skills Inventory. Does anything strike you about it? Any "ah-ha!" moments? Do you have 40 skills listed but realize you're only using five of them on any given day in your work? Did you run out of room on your paper and have to grab another sheet to keep listing all the skills you've acquired since you became a mom and an entrepreneur? Or did you discover some skills that have perhaps become strengths? For any items on your list you want to use more of in your work, consider how you can make that happen. For example, Lara has learned from doing her podcasts and TV interviews that she really enjoys working in and with the media, so she is actively seeking opportunities to do more coaching via television and radio platforms. Few people ever sit down and catalog their strengths and skills like this, and even fewer make the decision to purposefully incorporate their best talents into their everyday lives. But you've got the smarts and the guide right here to do it for yourself, and you'll be happy you did.

A Bonus Tool: Intuition

The last part of your toolkit is intuition—an often overlooked tool. As moms, we rely on our intuition to tell us if we need to be concerned about a new friend our child has made or a situation our child is (or isn't) telling us about. Intuition is mysterious but it's also very valuable, and because women are known to have a heightened sense of intuition, it would be silly of us not to put that to work for ourselves in the business world as well.

When it comes to intuition, do you listen to it? Do you value it? Or do you dismiss and ignore it? Sometimes we aren't even aware that we have ignored it until later, when we realize too late that our intuition was trying to tell us something. Sound familiar? For some reason, things that we can see, taste, touch, and smell are more often more valued in our society than things we simply feel. We can tell you, though, that we've worked with many women who wished they had listened to their gut, and we have worked with many who chalk up their success to trusting their gut when they truly had no idea how something would work out. Using your intuition can save you time, money, hassle, and heartache, so it's worth paying attention to.

Moms Talk

Don't operate out of a place of fear. Rely on your intuition. Rely on your own judgment. Operating from a place of fear will lead to bad decisions. Trust yourself.

—Cause Haun, See Kai Run

One thing that I've had to kind of make friends with is that I'm going to make a lot of mistakes and I'm going to learn a lot from them. The major mistakes I've made have been a result of questioning myself and looking outside of my instinct and my knowledge to others whom I perceive to be more knowledgeable, and trusting them versus trusting me.

—Sharelle Klaus, Dry Soda

Whether you are just starting out or have a well-established business, this chapter has offered another opportunity to true things up. Are there some tools in your toolkit you had forgotten about? Have you gained some new skills throughout the years you have had your company? For example, if you've recently expanded your team, maybe you've discovered you totally rock when it comes to managing and motivating people. Add that to your list of skills, or even add it to your strengths if you feel it's bigger than simply delegating and telling others what to do. Sometimes the skills we practice over and over do indeed become strengths or tap into some natural talents we never knew we had. In the example we just gave, the skills of managing people and being a good delegator could morph into a strength we call leadership. We are inviting you to acknowledge all your skills and talents now and evaluate how you can leverage them successfully in your business.

Bottom Line

- A mom entrepreneur's toolkit is made up of many different kinds of resources, many of which you may have forgotten you have.

- Even personality traits can be counted among your tools as a mom entrepreneur.

- As you grow in your business, it makes sense to occasionally reassess the contents of your toolkit to make sure you're using all the resources you have available to you.

- There is always an opportunity to increase, improve, or acquire new tools to support you as you grow.

Chapter 6

Business Planning

*I*t's time to take a close look at your business. Now that you have a clear understanding about who you are, what you want, how best to use your resources, and how you'll go about fitting it all in, you have to support your goals and dreams with some good old-fashioned planning. To do this, we'll start by having you complete an adapted version of the *One Page Business Plan*, which was created by Jim Horan, author of the best-selling One Page Business Plan series.[1] There are endless resources available about how to write a detailed business plan, and we encourage you to seek them out if, after completing this chapter, you want or need a more in-depth plan. In the meantime, consider this your big-picture plan—the one that helps you adopt the right mindset to create success on your own terms.

Of course, this is not the only business plan you'll need if you are seeking investors or creating partnerships. The plan you're about to create, though, is incredibly useful, and you will likely find that it's more than adequate to get you focused and send you on your way. For those of you who have been in business for a while, completing this plan or revisiting an earlier version you've made will still be very useful; in fact, our clients do their planning every year. It's great to set goals, measure your progress, and celebrate your success on an annual basis. Think of your business plan as a beacon to guide your decisions, and you will be so thankful you've taken the time to write it all down so you can stay on track and know how to make the right decisions for your business.

By the way, if you think for one minute that we're going to let you forget the unique challenges of being a mom when you are crafting your business plan, you are mistaken. As you answer these questions, keep in mind not just your business but your whole life. In fact, it's a good idea to have your answers regarding your values, priorities, motivators, and passions from Chapter 1 handy as you go through this exercise. You'll want to think about those things as you write your answers. After all, being a mom informs every area of your life, and that includes your plan for a wildly successful business that makes you happy.

Stages of Business

A cautionary note: Based on our experience working with mom entrepreneurs on business planning, we want you to know that it is incredibly common to have some pretty unreasonable expectations for your business, especially when you are just getting started. This can result in ineffective (and often disempowering) goal-setting. Sometimes this is caused by a lack of knowledge of the industry, or of the competition, or of what it takes to run and market a start-up company. Other times it's because you don't have a lot of experience setting SMART goals (we'll explain these in detail a little later in this chapter). Often, it's the result of a mom entrepreneur not knowing what to expect based on the stage her business is in.

To help you set appropriate and empowering goals, let's spend some time figuring out exactly which stage your business is in so you'll know what you can expect. We have a really fun way to help you understand where you are and what you'll need to do to move to the next stage: we're going to show you how the stages of business mimic the stages of pregnancy and child development. After all, how many times have you heard a mom entrepreneur refer to her business as her "baby"? (Maybe you do it yourself.) We create them, birth them, raise them, worry about them, celebrate them, and then one day send them on their way without us. You'll be surprised how much the stages of business development align with the stages of child development. Plus, we love how easy this analogy makes it to understand where you are and what you can realistically expect as you develop. Knowing where you are, what to expect, and what to focus on leads to "lightbulb" moments—at least it has for our clients, and we believe it will for you too.

Pregnancy

What to expect: This stage is full of hope and possibilities. You have an idea for a business, and your creativity is bursting. The possibilities are endless. This is the time to explore and imagine what can be. Ride the excitement, get your ideas down on paper, and let your thoughts and creativity roam where they may. You'll come up with a list of business names—some great, some awful—and you'll alternate moments of hyper-confidence that you'll be the next business scooped up on *Shark Tank*, with periods of doubt and fear that you will be an utter failure. You may love an idea for your business one minute and then hate it the next. That's normal. Don't get hung up on having it all figured out at this stage. Your job here is to grow your ideas, give them air, and see what develops.

(*A side note here:* You'll see that for each stage we include sample objectives for life and business all muddled together. This may seem a little disorganized, as we tend to want to put personal goals in one box and professional ones in another, but we are throwing them all in the same pot to illustrate the point that when you're a mom entrepreneur, your priorities have to commingle. It is messy. The lines are blurry.)

Sample objectives for this stage:

✎ Define your business: think about what you'd like to offer, who you think would most likely buy it, what sort of branding appeals to you, and how this business will leverage your strengths, skills, and style. How will it honor your priorities? How will it showcase the best of you?

✎ Figure out how your business will fit in the market and what makes you different from your competition.

✎ Set a target for where you want to be in your business and life in one year, two years, and five years, while considering what your family and lifestyle will be like at those points in time.

✎ Continue great self-care.

✎ Meet with other business owners to hear their stories, and to learn how they got started, what mistakes they made, and what they think of your ideas.

✎ Surround yourself with supportive friends and family.

✎ Find possible mentors to support you in this new adventure.

✎ Read *The eMyth Revisited* by Michael Gerber (and any other business books you can get your hands on).

✎ Attend workshops on starting and running a company.

✎ Accept offers of help.

✎ Set a launch or grand-opening date.

✎ Create a work schedule that works for your whole life.

Birth

What to expect: The business equivalent to birthing a baby is launching your business (or new product or service). The launch requires extreme focus, planning, and follow-through to make your idea a reality. It requires all of your time, effort, and energy, and will be exhausting at times. You'll want to focus on other things, take a break, and maybe even quit, but the launch requires you to keep going. You are, after all, following through on a huge commitment you've made to yourself, and the satisfaction of achieving your goal lies just on the other side of this hard work. You'll need a carefully crafted marketing strategy, sales process, delivery/fulfillment system, customer service plan, and follow-up program, to name just a few of the critical elements of a launch. Expect that many of these will be beyond your competence to handle, so plan on dumping your wallet on the nearest countertop and asking various freelancers and experts to take whatever they need to help you get the job done. Don't worry—paying for help at this stage is often necessary. You will learn a lot along the way so that you can cut expenses in future stages.

Sample objectives for this stage:

✎ Commit to and practice logging off the computer and/or phone when it's family time. Be present with your family when you're with them, and give work your focus during your planned office hours.

✎ Create a launch strategy to make your business visible to your target audience.

✎ Launch your branded website with Home, About, Services/Products, and Blog pages.

✎ Write the first 10 blog posts to populate your blog when the site is launched.

✎ Secure a babysitter or other childcare support so you have a certain number of hours per week to focus exclusively on your business.

✎ Commit to a monthly date night with your spouse or partner. Hire a babysitter for the third Thursday of every month (or whatever date works for you) as a standing event so you have no excuse to neglect your relationship.

✎ Attend networking meetings, conferences, and trade shows where your ideal clients are most likely to be. It is critical at this stage for you to become visible and credible to your target audience. If no one knows you exist, it's going to be hard to make money.

✎ Create a comprehensive daily, weekly, and monthly schedule (see Chapter 3) so you're clear about when you're able to work.

Infancy

What to expect: This stage of your business is a tough one. Just as a baby takes all your time, effort, and energy and gives you nothing in return (except the occasional smile that we live for), so goes this stage of business (sometimes minus the smiles). You have to constantly feed your business, pour all of your resources (time, money, focus) into it, and you can expect very little obvious payoff. You may wonder if you're doing the right thing and whether your efforts will ever be worth it. You'll likely grow tired of the constant work, and even though you know things will get easier at some point, it sure won't feel like it most of the time. This stage of business usually lasts anywhere from about six months to a year.

This stage is all about putting forth effort that will enable your business to mature. If you're successful, your business will indeed begin to show signs of growth. It's alive! That's about all the thanks you get at this point, though. This is not meant to bum you out; we think it's best to know that this is normal and necessary in order for your business to reach the next stage. Your mindset needs to be about focusing on your goals, following your plans, and staying in consistent action. You need to spend your efforts and money on being visible and credible to your market. Don't expect to see the money pouring in just yet.

Sample objectives for this stage:

- ✎ Create profiles on relevant social media networks—the ones your target audience uses.
- ✎ Pick a few school activities to participate in this year and block them off on your calendar

so nothing impacts them. Then ignore the rest of the requests you recieve to participate this year. You'll have time in later stages of the business to get more involved in your children's school days, but for now, leave the bulk of the volunteer opportunities to the parents who aren't running a brand-new business.

- Post daily on your social media networks. Build relationships with an audience, and those relationships will build your business.
- Blog weekly about topics that showcase your expertise.
- Infancy is a tough stage, so make self-care automatic by scheduling a massage (or pedicure or facial) in your calendar in advance. Then, while you're paying for the service, go ahead and schedule your next appointment.
- Attend virtual and in-person networking events each week/month to meet prospects.
- Rely on your network as needed for pick-me-ups and support.
- Follow up with warm leads every week.
- Reach a certain number of followers or likes on social media.
- Obtain endorsements on LinkedIn and testimonials for your Website.
- Send out product samples to promotional partners.

Toddlerhood

What to expect: Ever notice how toddlers zoom around, running into walls and falling down, but never really suffer major setbacks? It's almost like they're made of rubber, and we moms often scratch our heads in amazement that anyone ever survives this stage of development. In your business, toddlerhood is a fun time during which you start experimenting with different ideas. You'll tweak your offerings, your brand, and your target market as you learn more about what your audience wants from you and what you're best able to give them. You can try new and varied approaches, products, and markets with low risk for harm. You have started making money, you likely have some happy customers, and you have the feeling that this really is starting to look like a business, if you do say so yourself. It's not unusual to find that your business name or branding don't seem to fit anymore. This phase is all about growing, stretching, and trying new things. Experiment with different marketing strategies or ask past customers for feedback about what they would like to see from your company.

Your job in this stage is to explore and discover the lessons your business is teaching you now. You may evolve in your business, brand, and product line at this stage, and that is perfectly reasonable. You'll be making some money and attracting clients or customers, but probably still won't have a steady, reliable income. The clients you do have are helping you learn your strengths and helping you decide which type of clients and projects are ideal for you—and which ones are not. Adjust your goals and branding accordingly. This stage usually lasts from one to three years.

Sample objectives for this stage:

- ✎ Create a profile on a new social media channel with a marketing strategy to support it.

- ✎ Find and secure opportunities to speak in front of your target audience (usually for free at this point).

- ✎ Choose a leadership role in your child's school, sport, or club so you can experience something together. Coach soccer, be the room mom, help with Scouts, take an art class together, or sign up for a fitness program you and your child(ren) do together.

- ✎ Create and launch a new product or offering.

- ✎ Create a joint venture with a business that is not competitive with you but has the same audience.

- ✎ Now that you've left the infancy stage of your business, it's time to reconnect with friends. Make some time for a girls-only dinner or maybe even a getaway.

- ✎ Rebrand your business, update your logo or Website, or *true up* your messaging to match how your offerings or your audience may have evolved at this point.

- ✎ Grow your client base.

- ✎ Set a financial goal ("I will make $_____ by _____ date.").

✎ Plan a getaway or two. Maybe one family vacation and one couples-only, if you can swing it.

Adolescence

What to expect: This long, fun stage is a period of extremes. There will be days when you'll love your business and be thrilled with your success, and then there will be days when you don't like it at all and fear you're going to go under. The feast-or-famine cycle often sets in because you have enough customers or client work to keep you very busy, given your current planned work hours each week; but you neglect marketing, so when business slows down, you have to hustle to find new work or to sell more of your product. And because self-promotion doesn't come easily for most mom entrepreneurs, you will spend some time denying you have a marketing or sales problem and instead want to put your energy into developing new products or dreaming up new business ideas altogether.

However, just as our children have to learn the self-discipline required to allow them to take turns, sit in their desks at school, and get their homework done when they would rather play outside, all adolescent business owners need to discipline themselves to manage marketing their company while also running it and doing what it takes to make money.

Your pipeline begins to fill and stay full. You're making more money and recovering your start-up expenses. You'll begin reducing (or at least maintaining) your expenses while watching your income increase. You'll attract many opportunities, so you'll need to choose carefully to stay true to your brand rather than running with every possibility that presents itself. This is the point at which you want to check in to make sure that your business still reflects you. Once you get a bit of success, it's remarkably easy to turn off your inner knowing and succumb to pleasing others.

That's what almost happened to Andreea Ayers with the handcrafted soap company she started. She had loyal customers who loved her products, but her vision of success included being able to sell her soaps in Whole Foods markets. When the opportunity to do that finally came, she decided, surprisingly, to turn it down. Ultimately, it would have completely shifted her entire business model. "I realized that I don't want to be an employer," she told us. "I am happy being an entrepreneur, working with freelancers and having a small workspace." To meet the demands of having her soaps sold in Whole Foods, she would have had to shift from being an entrepreneur to an employer, and that didn't suit her.

Turn up the volume on what's most important to you in life and in business so that you can drown out the noise that would send you down a path that isn't right for you. When you're in this phase, it's a great idea to revisit the values, priorities, and motivations that you articulated in Chapter 1. They are the voice of reason during the adolescent phase of your business—similar to a parent's voice during a child's adolescence. Rely on them to keep you going in the right direction. In keeping with this idea, turn away non-ideal work and non-ideal clients. Enjoy the success. You've earned it. This stage lasts anywhere from about two to five years.

Sample objectives for this stage:

- ✎ Evaluate which tasks you need to continue doing in your business and which ones you can hire out.

- ✎ Consider school and extracurricular activities for your children and plug important dates into your calendar now.

- ✎ Hire an assistant or other staff so you can delegate certain administrative, fulfillment, or marketing tasks.

- ✎ Plan a family vacation and at least one couples-only getaway every year. Time away from work is critical to keep you motivated and well-connected with your family.

- ✎ Make strategic partnerships with the people, groups, and/or businesses that can help you reach beyond your current network of clients and prospects.

- ✎ Increase sales.

- ✎ Reduce expenses.

- ✎ Continue scheduling self-care on a regular basis so that you'll have the energy and mindset you need to continue running your business.

- ✎ If you are a service provider, raise your fees as needed.

✎ If you make consumer products, consider tar-
geting a new audience.

Teenagerhood

What to expect: You know that stage when your children start thinking they know everything? Although they
certainly can wow you at times with their smarts, they
also have no idea yet what they don't know. Well, this
stage is a lot like that. You are quite the expert in some
areas of your business, but the amount of time, effort, and
energy it takes to run it yourself is causing you to let a few
balls drop in other areas.

This long stage is all about improving your offerings, your marketing, and your processes. You're likely
to hit a plateau here because you are already doing everything you know how to do well. To get past this, attend
some conferences or workshops (maybe it's a good time
to learn about mobile marketing, for instance), or hire a
coach or mentor to help you learn what you don't know.
But don't stray from your core platform and offerings.
You're making good money and keeping your customers
happy. The goal here is to expand into new markets or
try out new delivery methods while staying true to what
you know works.

In the teen years, your brand is now a well-established
and trusted resource, so it's common that demand for your
offerings will begin to outpace your ability to deliver them
all by yourself. Say goodbye to the "I" and hello to the
"team"! This is the stage in which most mom entrepreneurs

are ready to begin outsourcing or bringing on employees, if you haven't already. Consider your strengths, as we discussed in Chapter 5. What parts of your business must you do? Which ones play to your strengths, feel easy for you, and make you money? At this stage of the business, it's time for you to "shake your money-maker" and offload other required business roles and tasks that

a. don't make you money,

b. aren't easy or fun for you to do (i.e., are not your strengths), and

c. could be done faster and better by someone else.

Moms Talk

When I was considering various ways to expand my soap company that wouldn't require me taking out huge loans, I started looking at ways to reduce costs. I could have shipped all the soaps myself and saved some money, but I get excited about marketing and selling, not about shipping.

—Andreea Ayers, Launch Grow Joy

It's time to shift your mindset from the "Chief Everything Officer" and start owning the title of "Chief Executive Officer" in your company. Your job at this stage is to be the visionary, to set the path and lead the team and the business. If you're still trying to do it all by yourself, you're setting yourself up for burnout and failure. You'll experiment with learning to manage people and multiple projects. You'll have to create processes that will allow you to successfully delegate work to those who support you. There will be successes and setbacks and a lot of late nights. It's all part of the stage.

Moms Talk

As I started traveling more and more to build my company and promote my brand, my children made it clear that they did not like it one bit! They told me that they didn't want me to keep flying away. Even when my trips dwindled down to only once a month and I personally felt like I was not traveling too much, they were still voicing their discontent. Clearly my traveling was affecting them more than I realized. Of course, my business needed me, as the face of the company, to travel. However, this was one of the things I had to figure out in terms of running a family business, and that was: what took priority. There are no hard and fast rules about how much PR and marketing is enough, or how much time your kids really need you, or how much damage you are doing by traveling. I had to determine for myself how to meet the needs of my family and my business at the same time.

My priorities helped me get creative. I started having employees and even enthusiastic customers (brand ambassadors) attend events that I normally would have so we could continue to increase our brand presence without it always having to be me. It did take a while to learn how to do this correctly, and obviously as my brand grew, I had more brand ambassadors to enlist. But I also sat my kids down and explained to them that I was making an effort to not travel as much as I used to, and that I had skipped a lot of trips they didn't even know about, choosing to stay with them instead. They had to understand that I did need to travel sometimes to grow my business. And "my business" is their business. So to sum it up, finding balance when your family is growing and your business is growing is a tough endeavor. It is a struggle, but the challenges have certainly helped shape my brand, and my family.

—Michal Chesal, Baby K'Tan

Sample objectives for this stage:

- ✎ Expand the experts on your team and delegate certain administrative, fulfillment, or marketing tasks.

- ✎ Does your job require you to travel on a regular basis? If so, discuss with your family how often this makes sense and how they can run the household in your absence. Consider hiring a nanny, if you need to. Conversely, cancel the nanny if the expansion of your work team allows you to step back into your mom and family manager roles in a bigger way.

✎ Continue to refine your regular processes in sales, marketing, and delivery. Look for ways to automate or improve the efficiency and reduce the cost of these systems.

✎ Create a standard operating procedure for each of these departments so you are more efficient and so you can confidently pass some of this off to your staff.

✎ Write or update your business plan for the next year.

✎ Book a conference, a workshop, or coaching sessions to help you determine what's next in your business.

✎ Take a leadership course.

✎ Make plans to do one of those things on your "someday" list—learn to play the piano, travel to that distant isle, train for a marathon, or sign up for language classes at the local college.

✎ Create compelling offerings for your past clients.

✎ Increase income and profitability.

✎ Reduce expenses.

✎ Reinvest $X back into the business each year.

✎ Invest in professional development and stay abreast of trends in your industry.

- ✎ Commit to an annual retreat with your girlfriends.
- ✎ Create at least one passive income stream.
- ✎ Consider introducing new products to round out your offerings.

Maturity

What to expect: The period after the teen years and leading toward maturity in your business is a unique, rather undefined one (just as it is with children). There are many different ways for your business to successfully grow up. This will greatly depend on how you have defined success for yourself—as we've mentioned, that's different for every mom entrepreneur. Some of our clients have chosen to license or franchise their companies; others have chosen to sell their mature business (or parts of it) to the highest bidder. Still others have told us they have no intention of expanding into an empire, because they enjoy the hands-on work and personal contact their business provides them. There is no right or wrong way to grow your business, and bigger isn't always better.

Some things to shoot for: Your business is completely functional without you. Even when you are on vacation, the company still thrives. You have an exit strategy in place, as the company no longer revolves around you and is now its own entity. You can choose to continue working in or on the company, but it is thriving and paying you back for all the years of blood, sweat, and tears you poured into it. You have a nice source of income you can rely on (or you sell it completely to another entity), regardless of the time you spend thinking about it.

Sample objectives for this stage:

✎ Work with your small-business attorney to create your exit strategy, if that's part of your plan.

✎ Have your business valuated.

✎ Discuss a five-year plan with your family. How old will the kids be? Where will they be in school? Is it time to move to a larger house or to downsize at this point?

✎ Evaluate your family's savings, assets, college funds, and retirement plans, and set goals to achieve the results you want.

✎ Designate your second in command, even if you aren't planning on quitting or selling the company, and have him or her fully trained in all aspects of the business.

✎ Look for strategic alliances that can boost sales or reach new markets.

✎ Check in with yourself and see whether your personal life is on track. What's next for you?

Moms Talk

When my daughter started our handmade toffee business back when she was in high school, we never dreamed it would turn into the business it did. I started helping her keep up with the business while she was in college, and then when she moved on and got a full-time job, I took over the daily operations. We use a family recipe that we carefully guard. I have no desire to sell this business or let some large production company take over, although we've had offers. I like personally overseeing every step of the process and being in the kitchen. It keeps me busy.

—Pat Stone, Bellstone Toffee

I've always been an artist, musician, and storyteller, and that has led me to venture into several businesses. I'm willing to take risks that some creative people are not willing to take when trying to find a way to make a living doing what they love to do. When it comes to Super Blanky, my blanket/superhero cape business, I have a patent-pending design. I'm getting great press and expanding my business. It's growing fast and starting to be more than I can keep up with by myself. I'm thrilled it is taking off, and am already considering the option of building the business with an exit strategy. While I love the product and the joy it brings to my customers, I don't have a problem letting it grow beyond me. Selling it would free me up to pursue other hobbies and businesses, or maybe create another new one.

—Karen Czarnik, Super Blanky

• • •

Success will be much easier to reach if you pick the right measurement for the stage you're in. We have seen so many mom entrepreneurs feel like giving up when they're only six months or a year into their business because they're not yet making money. Money seems to be the only metric many women focus on. They're doing everything they are supposed to be doing. They're following the textbook on networking, marketing, and sales, and they consume every bit of information they can find about running a small business. But if you're trying to measure the success of your infant company by the money you're making, you will probably feel like a failure. The same goes with expecting to replace your former corporate income within a year via a startup company you created that no one has ever heard of. Both of these scenarios make as much sense as expecting a toddler to sit quietly and take notes during a college lecture course. And yet many of our clients have exactly these misplaced expectations of themselves and their companies.

As with raising children, it can be hard to notice when you're outgrowing one stage and moving into another. It is definitely a gradual process, though it often feels like waking up to discover that your 3-year-old daughter has turned into a teenager overnight. Or that you're still laying out clothes for your 13-year-old son to wear each day when he's perfectly capable of doing that himself. What our children are capable of and what we can expect from them changes with every stage of child development. The same goes for your business. We hope this explanation will help you see both what's possible now and what you can look forward to in the future.

Your One-Page Business Plan

Now that you have determined which stage your business is in and what sort of objectives or goals make sense right now, let's roll up our sleeves and plug those goals into your One-Page Business Plan. Remember, our goal with this type of business plan is to help you create a vision for the success you want to achieve and the plan to get you there. If you don't fancy yourself a business planner, don't get scared off. Answering the questions we are about to present will create a path to help you get the success you envision. And this is only one page long. You can do one page of planning, can't you? We know you can. And doing so will get you in the right mindset to put your vision into action, and, most importantly, to just get started, which is often the hardest part.

This plan gives you a chance to think about what you do, why you do it, whom you serve, how the product or service is delivered, and what will make you successful with time. So let's get to it.

Hint: As we go through this planning exercise, it's helpful if you write down what comes to mind right away without editing yourself and then go back and spend a few minutes thinking about the question more thoroughly to see if anything else pops into your head. Go ahead and grab your pen and paper. At the top of it write "Business Plan." Write down the following questions in bold and leave space for your answers.

Here's an example of a completed One-Page Business Plan to give you an idea of how you answer the questions.

Sample Business Plan

Beautiful, artistic, usable everyday art for the kitchen and dining room. We curate and reclaim all sorts of vintage platters, bowls and dishes and create unique tiered serving dishes, wall art and centerpieces.

Vision

What are you building?

To bring art into the everyday and make beauty a part of the dining experience. And to provide an outlet for my creativity and my obsession with lovely dishes.

Mission

Why does this business exist?

- Launch website featuring my five categories of artwork (with five pieces each) by February 2015
- Book four trade shows for fall by March 2015
- Create 200 pieces for fall trade shows by August 2015
- Generate $12,000 in sales for first year
- Keep expenses below $2,500 in 2015

Objectives

What will you measure?

- Schedule working weekends to create the pieces
- Determine quantities of all supplies needed prior to each working weekend and have them on hand
- Hire copywriter to write compelling copy for Home, About, Products pages on website
- Choose best tradeshows in my region that target women 25-55

Strategies

What will make this business successful over time?

- Research top-ranked tradeshows in the region and select my four choices by March 2015
- Hire web designer by January 2015
- Hire copywriter by January 2015
- Have first 25 pieces professionally photographed by February 2015

Action Plans

What is the work to be done?

✎ **Vision: What are you building?** What is your business? What do you do? Whom do you serve? How do you deliver?

✎ **Mission: Why does this business exist?** What is your motivation for doing this work? How does this business fill a need in the market and a need/passion/desire in your life? What does it make possible that wouldn't happen otherwise?

✎ **Objectives: What will you measure so that you know it is successful?** This could be sales, number of products sold, Web hits, Twitter followers, income, or something else. Remember to figure out which goals make sense based on your stage of business. There is no point in setting unrealistic objectives, and we have given you a lot of sample objectives to get your wheels turning. Let's talk a minute about refining your goals so that they are as "SMART" as you are.

Most people know about SMART goals. They were introduced in the 1980s and the letters stand for:

Specific

Measurable

Attainable

Realistic

Time-related

Setting a SMART goal means you're setting specific, measurable goals rather than general ones. So instead of saying, "I want to make enough money to support my family," you need to define what "enough" is. A SMART way to state that goal is, "I want to earn an income of $85,000 in 2015." If we call you on January 1, 2016 and ask you if you achieved that goal, you will be able to answer with clarity that you met the goal, exceeded it, or fell short of it. More examples of SMART goals include, "Hire first three employees by March 2015," and, "Add four new products to product line by September 2016."

How about some personal goals? Lara has had this one on her business plan every year since 2009: "Put a healthy, home-cooked meal on the table by 6:30 p.m. five nights a week." Remember how we said we weren't going to forget about how your role as a mom informs every other part of your life, including your business? Well, that's exactly why Lara puts this goal in her business plan every year. She knows that if she allows her ambition to go unchecked, it can cause her priorities of health and quality family time to slip. And because she highly values eating home-cooked meals with her family, this goal keeps her priorities in check. It isn't exactly a business goal, but it is the kind of goal that supports the lifestyle of a mom entrepreneur. To that end, it's also a SMART goal in that it is specific and measurable.

Recently, we ran across a coach named Deborah Grayson Riegel who has her own variation on the meaning of SMART goals. She changed the letters a bit to get to this:

Shareable: You'll want someone to keep you accountable or someone who encourages you

Motivating: Something that excites you and everyone who will be involved in meeting the goal

Actionable: Can you do something toward the goal right now?

Resonant: Does it give you chills—either excited chills or freaked-out-but-in-a-good-way chills?

Timely: Is now the right time to get started?

Don't forget, goals are dreams with deadlines attached to them, so always be sure to list the date you expect to complete or achieve a goal. With all the tools we're giving you in this chapter, what objectives can you create so you can track and measure your progress throughout a specific amount of time? Read on so you understand the way Objectives, Strategies, and Actions work together in your business plan.

1. **Strategies: What will make this business successful in time?** For every objective you list, you will need to have a few strategies to ensure you reach the goals. For instance, if you want to book 12 speaking gigs for next year, you may need to work on building your visibility and credibility to your target audience so they are more likely to hire you. Strategies to accomplish this could include joining a speaker's bureau, mentioning your speaking topics across your social channels and in blog posts, and having interviews with the media on your speaking topics.

2. **Action Plan: What is the work to be done?** List the actions (or to-do list) for each of the strategies you have listed in the previous question.

You can just do a brain dump here, or you can be a bit more organized in your approach (which we recommend) by considering one objective at a time, then listing the strategies associated with that objective, and then creating your action plans (or to-do list) for each of your strategies. (See the next table illustrating how to break your objectives into strategies and action plans.) For instance, for the social-media mentions to attract more speaking gigs, you might have an action list including writing a blog post about your speaking topics each week and posting relevant quotes related to your speaking platform across Facebook, Twitter, LinkedIn, and so on. It might make your simple business plan a little longer if you drill down this way, but the extra effort will be worth it.

Objective –> Strategies –> Action Plans

Let's take the example we mentioned of the mom entrepreneur who wants to increase her paid speaking opportunities. She has an objective to book 12 speaking gigs in 2015. Follow along as we drill down on how to break that objective into relevant strategies and how to assign action plans to each strategy.

SAMPLE OBJECTIVE:
Book 12 speaking gigs in 2015

Strategy #1: Register with speaker's bureau	Strategy #2: Update Website/ online presence to showcase me as a speaker	Strategy #3: Secure media placements interviewing me on my platform/ topics of expertise
Actions for This Strategy	**Actions for This Strategy**	**Actions for This Strategy**
Research top speaker's bureaus in my industry	Update "About Me" page of Website to include mention of speaking	Create media "one sheet" for press inquiries/ pitches
Ask friends for recommenda-tions/endorse-ments of my speaking abilities	Create media kit with my best speaking topics (include professional headshot, link to sizzle reel)	Register account with HARO (Help a Reporter Out) to watch for appropriate opportunities to feature my content and get interviews

Create sizzle reel of me speaking to send to bureaus	Add "Speaking" to list of services and give clear direction on Website about how to make inquiries about hiring me	Look for PR opportunities (on HARO and other sites) and queries on my platform. Pitch timely topics related to current trends, hot topics, seasons, etc.
Choose speaker's bureau and submit my application	Update all social profiles (LinkedIn, Twitter, Facebook, YouTube, Google Plus, etc.) to include and reflect my services as a professional speaker	Create list of 10–20 relevant blogs to which I'd like to contribute an article
	Update e-mail signature to include title of "Speaker"	Connect with those bloggers (and some of their readers) via social media to begin building relationships before I pitch them

	Blog/post tips, quotes, funny stories, etc., on social media channels relevant to my speaking topics to build awareness that this is my expertise	Pitch selected bloggers

An action plan similar to this is the best way to avoid being busy all the time without getting results to show for it. And we know that you don't have time to waste. Many of us enjoy creating to-do lists and marking things off as we get them done, but an action plan like this is even better because you can see exactly how your actions are leading you to the results you want.

And, because we strongly believe that having a meaningful purpose for your work is crucial both in moving you toward your goals and in keeping you going when the going gets tough, let's make that a part of your planning too. Review your answers from the vision exercise in Chapter 2 and, based on those or any other aspirations you have toward meaningful work, see if you need to add anything to your business plan. For example, if contributing to society is part of your vision, what strategies and actions could you include that will allow you to contribute in some way? Perhaps you could give back a portion of your profits, or you could spend a set number of hours each month mentoring aspiring entrepreneurs. Believe it or not, linking business objectives, strategies, and tasks with something you feel strongly about personally can be very motivating and help drive you toward the business you envision.

When you have answered these questions, what you have may not look as in-depth as a typical business plan, but rest assured you will have created a strong understanding of the most important aspects of your business and what you need to do to move forward. If you would like to also complete a more in-depth traditional business plan (and we think you should go through that exercise at some point), there are a lot of books, organizations, and online resources to help when you're ready.

• • •

Congratulations, you're done! With your one-page business plan you have laid the foundation for a successful business endeavor. Whether you sell a product or a service, whether you are a solo entrepreneur, have a partnership, or have employees, and whether you are already established or are just exploring the possibility of starting your own company, the work you do here will help you create success on your own terms.

This plan may start to feel overwhelming. When you are first starting out, either with your whole business or with a new product or service, that's normal. Just remember the old saying, "When eating an elephant, take it one bite at a time." We still aren't sure why the person who originally said this chose an elephant, but you get the point: for large undertakings, you have to chip away at them. You have to take them one step at a time. And even though they're small, baby steps will indeed get you there.

We know it's hard. We know there are a lot of decisions for you to make, and we know those decisions have huge ramifications, which can make you feel paralyzed. We hope that this chapter has helped you get clear on the steps you need to take and the order in which to take them. These stages and their action items work for the development of most businesses, but we'd like to remind you that there are no absolutes. Because we are big on challenging the rules, especially the ones you make up yourself and then feel obligated to adhere to, we don't want to add any more rules for you to follow. So use these stages as a general guideline for what you can expect and where you will most likely spend your time and energy. Then, of course, check in with yourself along the way to make sure what you are doing is right for you.

Bottom Line

- ✎ You'll have more reasonable expectations and be better able to meet them if you know which stage of business your company is in.

- ✎ A simple business plan that allows you to state your vision, your motivation, and your goals is a powerful tool for a mom entrepreneur.

- ✎ A carefully crafted business plan is a critical success factor for all business owners.

- ✎ A plan ensures that your actions are aligned with your business purpose, helps you monitor your progress, and lets you right yourself or change direction if things go awry.

Chapter 7

Productivity Tools

*N*ow that you have designated the time you have available for your business, you have completed your business planning, and you are clear on your objectives and next steps, it's time to put all of that to work for you. We talked about using your time wisely in Chapter 3; in this chapter we'll dive into it more, with the goal of increasing your productivity. The most important thing to remember—and to own—as you get started is the fact that you are both a mom and an entrepreneur. We've said this before but it's important to remember because your time is likely more limited, your schedule is likely more variable, and your priorities are likely a bit different from those of some other business owners. As you design your days, your weeks, and your months, you need to be sure you are also keeping in mind all of your commitments, obligations, and priorities.

Because time is a limited resource that can greatly impact how quickly you'll progress toward your goals, it makes sense to get a good handle on how best to use it. First, we'll look at some common stumbling blocks when it comes to time. These are the things that can get in your way. Luckily, they are all within your control and fairly easy to manage.

Lack of Boundaries

Setting boundaries around your time is incredibly important. Other people can certainly impinge upon your boundaries, but it's likely that *you* are the major culprit getting in your own way in this regard. Here is the solution in a nutshell: When you've scheduled time to work, let yourself work. The unscheduled calls coming in to your cell phone can wait. By answering the phone, you are letting someone else decide how you spend your time. If you work from home, the laundry can wait. By folding the laundry during work hours, you are sending yourself the message that those towels are more important than your business objectives. Even Facebook can wait. Seeing all of the great things that other people are doing does not in any way help you do your own great things. Yes, the call deserves your future attention, you are going to want folded towels at some point, and we're all for catching up on what everyone on social media is up to, but those things do not need to happen during the precious time you've set aside for your business. (One caveat: You may be using social media to connect with your audience. If so, be sure to observe the boundaries between doing work on social media and playing on social media. Both are great but they need to be done at the appropriate times.)

Distractions and Interruptions

Take a minute to think about the distractions and interruptions that show up on a regular basis. Write down what they are, and write down a plan to deal with them.

Think: texts, phone calls, social media, e-mails, the sale at Banana Republic, and so on. (By the way, redrawing your boundaries can take some time. While you get a bit stricter with yourself, it's a good idea to notice when you are distracted. Distractions usually happen either because we fail to limit our exposure to them or because we need a break. Learn to notice the difference. We talked about energy levels and how they affect your ability to be productive in Chapter 3. If you do indeed need a minute, instead of scolding yourself, go replenish yourself and come back ready to roll up your sleeves and get back to work.)

Doing It All Yourself

How are you at delegating? How about automating? As the head honcho, it's easy to fall into the trap of thinking you have to do everything yourself. Whether you are a solo entrepreneur or the head of a large corporation, doing it all by yourself just doesn't make sense. Sometimes it comes down to money, of course, but there are creative ways to help you get around that. More often, it's not feeling ready to relinquish your control and trust that someone else will do things as well as you can. As we talked about in Chapter 5, you'll be better off if you can use your skills and strengths as often as possible. Of course, that means minimizing the time you spend doing things you either don't like that well or aren't good at. That doesn't mean you get to hand over the reins to another person and not check in with them from time to time. A powerful CEO carefully trains and checks in with her team and constantly reviews her automated processes to make sure things are running smoothly. Of course, getting things set up will take some initial time, but you'll get that time back—and then some—once you've cleared off some of your to-dos and can focus on the things that you do best as well as the things that are best for your company.

By the way, virtual assistants (commonly known as VAs) are an amazing and affordable resource. Think about some tasks you could either automate or delegate, and check out "22 Things You Can Outsource to a Virtual Assistant" in the Appendix if you need some ideas.

Resistance to Change

Next up on our list of things that hinder productivity: the fact that many of us are resistant to change. That's true when it comes to the route we take to work and the way we wear our hair. It's also true when it comes to your business and what we affectionately call "the way you've always done it." The way you've always done it can be great. Maybe it's the most efficient way to do it. Maybe it's a boon to your productivity. If that's true, great. More power to you. However, it might be worth considering that the way you've always done it could use a tweak or two. The thing is, technology is changing everything. Think of any issue or tasks in your business and we can almost guarantee that there is an app or piece of software that can help streamline it. So be open to new ways of doing things that might just increase your productivity.

Estimating Your Time

Ah, time again. Incorrectly estimating both how much time you need and how much time you think you have are common stumbling blocks as well. First, let's talk about underestimating the amount of time something will take. This is one of those things that just gets easier the longer you've been in business and the more you've done similar tasks. That said, estimating time naturally comes more easily to some than to others. If you notice that tasks consistently take longer than you thought they would, you might be someone (we'll call you a time optimist) who always believes she can get things done faster than she really can. Signs that you fall into this camp include never leaving enough time to get places, over-scheduling yourself because you forget to factor in traffic or bathroom breaks or the need to eat, and failing to notice that your weekly meeting that's scheduled from 9 to 10 a.m. always adjourns at 10:30. If any of these sound familiar, you'll need to make some adjustments to how you estimate the amount of time you'll need to get something done.

If you spent time in the corporate world and/or if your business is home-based, you might be especially prone to the second estimating issue: overestimating the amount of time you have to work. That's because when you are actually in an office setting, it's generally easier to focus on just work. Remember those distractions we were talking about? If you are working from home, it's all too easy to quickly throw a load of clothes in the washing machine or unload the dishwasher. We actually think these things can be perks of working from home, but be careful, because they can also eat into your productive time. Just be really honest when you are planning your days. If you know that you're the type to tidy up a bit during the day and you decide that's time well spent, make sure you schedule in time during the day to do those things.

Here's an example of how it doesn't make sense to schedule eight hours' worth of work each day if you don't have eight hours to work: A few years ago one of our clients came to a coaching session frustrated and overwhelmed. She was a hard worker and truly believed she was giving a 100-percent effort in everything she did for her clients and her family. But no matter how hard she worked day after day, she just couldn't complete her work projects and was starting to drop the ball and miss deadlines. She couldn't sleep at night, given the anxiety she felt about her work-load. To see what was happening, we had her track how she spent her time every day for a week. She was simultaneously shocked and relieved to finally see that despite starting her workday morning at 6:30 and working as hard as she could all day long, her family commitments (as a mother of preschool-aged children living in a rural area of Canada) were taking up all but about three hours a day. No wonder the eight hours' worth of projects wasn't getting done. The lesson in this story might seem obvious, but we can assure you that many of the mom entrepreneurs we work with have exactly the same disconnect between the time they have available to work and the amount of work they schedule on a given day.

As a mom entrepreneur, you are bound to feel frustrated if, day after day, you fall short of your goals. You may be pulling out your hair and questioning your abilities. The solution is to reset your expectations and plan projects that will fit into your timeframe. After doing that, instead of feeling completely overwhelmed and frustrated, you will likely find that you are able to meet your goals and feel quite productive. Make your schedule realistic and sustainable and you'll be on your way to feeling productive at the end of each day.

Techniques

Now that you are aware of the things that zap your productivity, let's look at a few tools to help you increase it. The rest of this chapter will lay out some techniques for productivity that will make a real difference in the way you feel about your days—especially if you fall into the category of those who look at the clock and think, *How is it already 7 o'clock?*

Chunk It

One popular time-management method is called the Pomodoro Technique. This technique is based on the idea that frequent breaks actually make you more productive. If you want to try it, the steps are simple:

1. Set a timer for 25 minutes, and work during that time.

2. Take a short (3- to 5-minute) break to do something unrelated to the task you are working on.

3. Set the timer for another 25 minutes, and then take another short break.

4. After four of these cycles, called "Pomodoros," take a longer (20- to 30-minute) break.

This technique can be tailored to suit your needs, but we find it's helpful to think of your total available time in "chunks" of some sort. Lara prefers to work in two-hour chunks with breaks between each chunk, because the idea of taking a break every 25 minutes would impact her ability to stay focused. Experiment with different chunks of time. Try working until you notice your mind wandering or until you start to feel antsy. Note how long you were able to stay on task, take a break, and then set the timer for that same chunk of time again. Tweak it until you find a rhythm that works well for you.

Map It

Another clear and proven method for managing time and also increasing productivity is something we call project mapping. In its simplest form, project mapping is plugging tasks from a project into the available time slots on your calendar. The first step is to determine the different parts of the project and how much time each will take. For example, if you need to write a blog post, you might need to spend 20 minutes figuring out your topic, 30 minutes writing it, five minutes coming up with a title, and five minutes posting it. Because the whole project will take an hour, you can look for an hour-long time slot on your calendar or you can find periods that fit with the different tasks within the project—in this case, a 20-minute time slot, a 30-minute time slot, and two five-minute time slots. Then, you schedule those specific tasks on your calendar. Simple, right? This can also work for huge tasks such as getting new retail accounts. Again, you'd break the project into smaller tasks and schedule each of those tasks on your calendar. Based on the size of the project, you may find that you need to add designated work time by working late a few nights or bumping some other activities from your calendar until the project is complete.

Calculate It

This leads us to a simple method of increasing productivity that has to do with choosing what gets on your calendar in the first place. It seems so obvious to do the things that have the most impact and get you closer to your goals, but we're guessing that you do a lot of things that don't fit that description. The Pareto principle, or, as it's commonly known, "the 80/20 rule," deems that in any situation, 20 percent of whatever you are talking about is vital and 80 percent of whatever you're talking about is trivial. For our purposes, it means that 20 percent of what you do leads to 80 percent of your progress. In simpler terms, you'll get the most benefit from doing the most important 20 percent of your tasks. If you really stop to think about it, we bet you'll see the wisdom in this. (And, if you want to apply this to other areas of your life, you probably wear 20 percent of your clothing 80 percent of the time, and in the sales world, it's often said that 80 percent of your income comes from 20 percent of your clients.) The takeaway? Figure out what your 20 percent is and focus on that.

Quarter It

Check out the following table: **The Four Qs of Productivity.** Here, we have divided our tasks into four quadrants. Each quadrant has several tasks most mom entrepreneurs need to do each day. Q1 (Quadrant 1) is full of the tasks you do that make you money. Q2 should include a list of items that fill your sales pipeline with income-generating opportunities (such as all marketing activities). Q3 tasks don't make money but must be done. These are the operations that keep your business going and the lights on. And Q4 is the quadrant where you put all the other stuff that winds up on your to-do list but that can usually be delegated or deleted from your task list altogether.

Grab a pen and paper and write out your own Four Qs of Productivity.

Challenge yourself to put at least five tasks in Q1 and Q4. It's usually fairly easy for a mom entrepreneur to fill in Q2 and Q3. Now, practice spending 80 percent of your time doing the tasks that fall in Q1 and Q2, and only allow 20 percent of your time to be spent on Q3. Notice you're out of time to do much of anything in Q4? That's right. You need to get those time drains off your list so you can be a productivity rock star.

The Four Qs of Productivity

Q1: Make $$$	Q2: Build $$$
• Selling products/ classes/packages of services • Client deliverables • Speaking • Consulting	• Marketing • Follow-ups/customer service • Networking • Social media • Blogging
Q3: Must-Do	**Q4: Time Sucks**
• Product development • Accounting • Administration • Team meetings • Learning • Training team	• Surfing the 'net • Updating your Website (unless you're a Web designer) • Socializing on social media (non-business-related) • Tweaking something until it's perfect

Besides the noble art of getting things done, there is the noble art of leaving things undone.
—Lin Yutang

Time It

Timing is a huge factor in determining how productive you can be as a business owner (especially when you're also a mom). Let's take another look at energy through the productivity filter. Consider your energy flow. Are you an early bird or a night owl? Does your energy wane every day after lunch? Do you constantly have the best ideas at 10 p.m.? It makes sense to pay attention to your biorhythms and use them to your advantage. Lara used to schedule teleseminars and Webinars in the evenings, thinking she'd be able to reach more of her target audience (moms) at that time. The problem was that once she put her kids to bed, her brain basically turned off. Trying to work in the evenings just doesn't work for her. She lacks the clarity that she has during the day, and each task ends up taking five times as long. Obviously, that is not time well spent.

As we mentioned earlier, scheduling your work time into chunks can really boost productivity. However, we know a lot of entrepreneurs who like to do marathon productivity blasts. Instead of clustering or chunking their tasks by the hour, they prefer to chunk their tasks by the day. For example, they may spend all day Monday on self-care, relaxing, de-stressing, and filling up their tanks with quality time spent by themselves, with their partner or kids, or with their friends. Then on Tuesday, they spend their entire day on their Q1 activities. In other words, they make a lot of money on Tuesday. And that's a nice way to spend a whole day. Wednesday is a catch-up day that allows for Q2 and Q3 tasks, and then they start the cycle, over.

You might follow a traditional five-day workweek or you might not. We know you are juggling work, running your household, and caring for your kids, among 5,000 other things. Tap into the timing that allows you to be the most productive you can be so your precious time is well-spent.

Question It

For all of those tasks that get bumped from Tuesday to Wednesday to Thursday, check in to see if the task is worth doing at all. "Do I want to do it? Do I have to do it (Q3)? What goal does this help me move toward (Q1 or Q2)? Which priority is positively impacted by doing it?" If you are able to answer these questions, and the answer seems to be that the task is worth doing, here are two last questions for you to consider: "What would make it easier or more appealing? When is the drop-dead due date?" Write the task on your calendar and don't let yourself wiggle out of it again. The tasks that keep getting pushed to the bottom of your lists take up a lot of mental energy that would be better spent elsewhere. Not doing something at all is actually a great way to see your productivity go up (and also to free up some time).

Maximize It

Another technique is to group tasks so that you can minimize transition times. Every time we move from one task to another, we lose valuable time because it takes our mind time to change focus. That's why it's pretty smart to group similar tasks together so that you are tackling them one after the other. If you need to make sales calls, set aside enough time to make them all (or at least several of them in a row). You'll benefit from the practice that comes with the repetition. If you need to write blog posts, write a few at a time. If you are going to be out visiting clients, make sure to visit all of the ones who are geographically close to one another. If you make a phone call, answer two e-mails, research something, and then make another call, it's likely that you're losing time transitioning from one task to another. Instead, group the similar tasks together so you can leverage your momentum.

Plan It

Successful entrepreneurs take the time to prepare for the next day by making a plan that allows them to hit the ground running. *We know, we know*—you probably work until the last second before you have to rush out the door to do carpool, or you work late into the night and just can't wait to turn off your laptop and hop into bed. We get it. We are here to tell you, though, that the time you take setting yourself up for the next day will be time well spent. Besides, it only takes a few minutes. Look at your calendar first to see what appointments you have and to get a feel for the time you have available, and then write down specific tasks that you want to do the next day. **Hint:** Rather than jotting down broad areas like "work on marketing," be specific ("identify five potential clients and send them an introductory e-mail") so you can hit the ground running.

Break It

As counterintuitive as it may seem, taking a break is actually a very effective way to be more productive. According to a study published in the *Journal of Consumer Psychology*, giving yourself a break helps you come up with solutions to your problems.[1] When you hit a wall or face an issue that seems insurmountable, walking away from things can actually allow you come up with a fresh perspective or find the answer you've been looking for. Take a shower. Go on a walk. Just do something that takes your mind (at least consciously) off the issue you are dealing with.

Focus It

Here's another technique for you that can work wonders: narrow your focus. This means to put all of your energy into only the most pressing activities or projects. There are times when a broad focus makes a lot of sense. For example, when you have established your business, you have had some success, and you are in a stable mode, you are likely focusing on sales, marketing, distribution, and customer relations all at the same time. Each of these categories gets some of your attention. There are other times, though, when you'll need to focus more narrowly so you can get done what you need to get done. For example, while we were writing this book, our focus became pretty darned narrow. We did the bare minimum to keep our businesses healthy but we pretty much stopped the extras because the book needed most of our attention. (Doesn't this remind you of times when one of your children is going through a period when he or she needs you? You almost automatically let some less-important things slide to the back burner.) When we promote the book, the focus will be much broader and will include our goals for our businesses. There are certain stages and periods in the life of your business when the focus will need to be narrow and times when the focus will need to be much broader.

Moms Talk

Something I have learned but still need to remind myself of is that stress does not equal productivity. I am usually able to get as much, if not more, accomplished when I am calm and methodically move through my checklist for the day or week. I also remind myself that I am not superhuman, and can only do what I can do without losing my mind.

—Kea Rensch, Merin Totes

When you're running a business from home you need to be ruthless with your time. Otherwise you'll find yourself burning the candle at both ends, which is a detriment to yourself and your business. Being organized is a must. Take time each night to plan your next day out. This will allow for you to quickly get started and keep the focus on revenue-generating activities. There are many different time-management applications and systems to use, but the important thing is to have some sort of system in place.

—Holly Hanna, The Work at Home Woman

My favorite strategy for maintaining productivity is to stay relatively busy. When I was in college, I worked every quarter except one. That quarter, I received dismal grades. I found that by having to closely manage my time, I had no choice but to use the time when I wasn't in class or working to get my homework and projects completed. I have found this to be true in my entrepreneurial life as well. I schedule out chunks of time for work, volunteering, and fun, and it makes me much more productive. Also, it seems like something unexpected comes up every day, so I make sure to schedule in at least an hour of flex time.

—Julie Fry, Business Among Moms

• • •

Productive equals effective plus efficient. Being effective means doing the right thing, and being efficient means doing it quickly. Doing something quickly when it's the wrong thing to do won't increase your productivity, so check in with your objectives and make sure you're spending your time doing the right stuff. And don't fall into the trap of thinking that you have to be productive every minute of the day. That's the exact attitude or mindset that makes some entrepreneurs turn into workaholics, and you can bet their overwhelm cycles kick in and make them miserable. With all the self-care hacks we shared with you in Chapter 4, we're sure you can manage being productive without sacrificing your well-being.

Make sure you give a few of these productivity tips a try when you feel you're stuck or spinning your wheels. And be aware that you probably have some longstanding habits that are zapping your productivity. We all do. It may take some time to change them, but start with taking some baby steps with the tips we've provided here.

We can't leave this chapter without saying that even with the best-laid plans, you will get off track now and then. Your son will get sick. Your daughter will need a last-minute costume or poster board. Expect to be waylaid on a somewhat regular basis, and perhaps even build that into your schedule. We've found that adding in a buffer when you create your calendar is almost always a good idea. Best case? You'll have more time than you scheduled for yourself. Worst case? You'll still have time to work and make the cookies that you just found out you are supposed to deliver to the bake sale this evening. We'll talk more about staying on track and getting back on track in Chapter 8.

Bottom Line

✎ The best gift you can give yourself as a busy mom entrepreneur is being productive with your time.

✎ Watch for common stumbling blocks that routinely zap your productivity.

✎ Try out some of the productivity techniques we included in this chapter to see what works best for you.

Chapter 8

Staying on Track

*B*y now we hope you clearly understand which stage of business you're in and what comes next. You have taken a close look at what you want for your future and you have a simple but powerful business plan in place. You've identified what's in your toolkit so you can potentially shorten your path to success and make the time spent reaching your vision more enjoyable. You are clear on your priorities and your values so you have a built-in way to make decisions and choose the best way to move toward what you want. You have taken ownership of your time and how to spend it.

So you can consider this business a future success, right? Oh, wait. We almost forgot something about you.

You are human, and we humans often need more than inspiration, more than a well-mapped-out schedule, but more than just know-how. Inspiration is everywhere, and, alas, it often doesn't last. Knowing what makes you tick and having a clear vision of your future definitely helps but it doesn't guarantee you'll take action on your plan. Furthermore, schedules are ultimately mere suggestions written on paper, on your computer, or somewhere on the Internet—suggestions that go by the wayside when life interrupts, as it often does.

No matter what your definition of success, focused action that leads to desired results equals fulfillment. That sounds easy enough, right? But what if the action part of that equation isn't happening? In other words, what if you know what you should be doing, but for some reason you aren't doing it? We are all vulnerable to things in life that get in our way and keep us from staying on track toward our goals. When you're a mom and a business owner, dealing with constant distractions, interruptions, unexpected events, and general chaos just comes with the territory. So let's include all of this in our expectations rather than allowing ourselves to get lost or stuck when the inevitable happens. Of course, there will also be times when an event, circumstance, or realization brings about total upheaval in your plans. In this chapter, we'll take a look at why that happens and help you figure out what to do next.

Obstacles

Let's start with understanding what gets in the way of following our plans on an average day (aside from the kids, the clients, your partner, your employees, your friends, and your neighbors all needing something from you). We have discussed in Chapters 3 and 7 some helpful ways to manage your time and be more productive. Some of these obstacles are in our control and others aren't. The most common obstacles that knock mom entrepreneurs off track include:

- ✎ Inspiration/innovation overload (something we call TIKEs, which we'll explain shortly)
- ✎ Mistakes
- ✎ Ruts
- ✎ Fear
- ✎ Failure

Let's start with the common obstacles that you can predict and prepare for.

TIKEs

How often have you gotten inspired and motivated by going to a workshop or reading a book, only to find that your inspiration fizzles a day or two later? Or perhaps you had a meeting with a colleague and had one of those lightbulb moments of clarity on exactly the new product to create or business to launch. Or what about when you have so many exciting plans floating around in your head after a meeting that you can't wait to get started, but six months later you still haven't done anything meaningful with them? That's TIKE (appropriate for moms, right?): Temporary Innovative Knowledge Euphoria. You get caught up following your thoughts and then eventually notice you've strayed far off the path.

In fact, this book has the potential to lead you straight into a TIKE moment. You're making plans. The plans are exciting. It all seems so doable. And then you put down this book, it slips under your bed, and before long, your schedule becomes a series of days that are, in essence, reactions to whatever is thrown your way. As a breed, entrepreneurs are constantly vulnerable to TIKE strikes. After all, we tend to highly value creativity, imagination, and innovation, and these are some of the exact qualities we count on to make our companies successful. However, these same characteristics can make it hard for us to follow through and execute on all those good ideas.

As coaches, we couldn't in good conscience leave you with a long list of to-dos and business ideas swirling in your head without also providing tools and techniques to deal with them. After all, Insight plus Action equals Results, and results will only happen if you take the action. Insight in and of itself doesn't have much effect at all, as you've likely discovered a week or two after attending the aforementioned workshop or reading the aforementioned book. We aren't talking about this book, though, because *Moms Mean Business* takes you past the inspiration phase and into action. In fact, one of the biggest factors that inspired us to write this book was the thought of helping mom entrepreneurs get past these TIKE strikes. Read on.

Mistakes

Talk about something we'd all love to avoid. Have you ever made a mistake that made you want to just retreat? You sent a proposal to the wrong person or you missed a critical deadline with a client? These are the types of errors that can throw you off your game and make you want to go curl up in a fetal position. You will make mistakes, and we're here to tell you that they can actually be very good things. Mistakes teach us and they make us stronger. The trick is to fix what went wrong to the best of your ability, assess what led to the error, learn from it, and move on. If the mistake went out into the world for others to see, owning up to the error shows that you are human. When you are vulnerable and admit what you don't know, it allows people to relate to you, and that's a good thing.

Moms Talk

The mistakes I've made with MomCom have forced me to evaluate what I need to change, what works and what doesn't, what I need to grow, and who and what deserves my energy. It has helped me focus on how I want to live my life. I count those as huge successes.

—Trish Morrison, MomCom

Ruts

Rut. Even the sound of it is pretty awful. When you find yourself stuck in one, it can be hard to find your way out. It happens when you've hit a wall or when you've run out of steam. In the physical fitness world, they call it a plateau. Perhaps you aren't making the same amount of progress you're used to or you aren't sure what to do next. Whatever the reason for getting stuck in the rut, you'll probably feel compelled to get out of it as soon as you can. Hold on for a second, though—there might be a lesson here. Before you start scrambling to get out of it, have a look around to see what the rut might be able to teach you. A rut can be an indication that something needs to change. It can be trying to show you that you need to think about moving in a different direction. It can help you see that you have unrealistic expectations. Look for the lesson, if there is one, and then you can begin to find your way out.

Great ways to get out of ruts include asking for help from a mentor, making a decision that's been looming over you, or checking in with your vision or your self-care needs. Getting stuck in a rut sometimes happens due to habits and routines we've created. You know the habits and routines we told you can help make you productive and successful? As helpful as they are, sometimes they can cause you to get stuck. In that case, shaking things up a bit with simple changes, like moving your laptop to a different room or taking a different route to the office, can help. A little change goes a long way.

Fear

Up next on our menu of things that can throw us off track is fear. Fear can show up in a lot of different ways, such as resistance to doing what you know you need to do. It can show up in the rules we've mentioned before (all those *shoulds* and *supposed tos* that stress us out). Fear can also result in something we call "imposter syndrome," which we describe as feeling out of sorts upon stepping into new territory. This is especially true when you or your business have just made a huge leap forward. For example, when we first signed our publishing contract, we both went through a bit of imposter syndrome. *Who are we to be writing a book?* we thought. *What do we know about the subject? Why would anyone listen to us?* Imposter syndrome struck in a big way and we had to deal with it.

Just remember, fear is best dealt with head-on. Scared to write? Go write. Scared to make a sales call? Make five of them. Whoever said the letters in *fear* stand for False Expectations Appearing Real was one smart cookie. Fear is something we all feel, but that doesn't mean what we fear is real, and it certainly doesn't mean that we have to stop what we are doing to pay attention to it. It doesn't deserve more than a few minutes of our attention, so acknowledge it and move on.

If you hear a voice within you say "you cannot paint," then by all means paint, and that voice will be silenced.
—Vincent Van Gogh

Failure

You put forth your best effort and it just wasn't enough. You went after a big sale and received a big no. You said you'd speak at a conference and weren't at all happy with how it went. The key here is not to mistake failing with being a failure, as they are two very different things. Failing is actually a pretty important part of success, and knowing you are going to fail from time to time, that it is inevitable, will help you weather the failures as they happen. This is not a permanent state, and we can guarantee that you will get over it. In fact, business and leadership experts tell us we should seek to "fail fast" in order to get the lessons we need to move forward.

Moms Talk

My husband loves to say, "If it was easy then everyone would be doing it." I took some huge risks when I decided to expand MomCom. I sold our rental house, which had significant sentimental value to us and was also our daughter's first home, to fund that business expansion. That was one of the biggest risks I've ever taken. It was difficult and uncomfortable, but doable. So it was a huge blow when the actual revenue from the business was much lower than the projected revenue, and then the money and the rental house were gone. I couldn't sleep at night and I was heartsick and physically ill knowing that I had to keep going forward with the big event I was planning. No matter how much I believed in my vision, it just was not going to work out the way I had planned. I put my heart, my money, and a huge part of my life on the line, and I lost.

—Trish Morrison, MomCom

Problems in business and life are like puzzles to solve. As you solve them you learn and grow and become better. Success to me is knowing that you live your life with integrity and use your gifts to create and contribute in some way.

—Veronica Bosgraaf, PURE Bar

Facing the challenges head-on will help you grow as both a person and a business owner. Being prepared for obstacles such as these will minimize the amount of disruption they cause. And when they can't be avoided? Look hard for a lesson you can take away as the reward for your efforts. We're trying hard to help you avoid sabotaging yourself when these obstacles show up, and you can bet they will.

• • •

We've given you some simple solutions to deal with the specific obstacles that you encounter, but now let's talk about the most effective tool we know of when it comes to staying focused and achieving our goals: accountability.

Accountability Techniques

Accountability is about keeping you in focused action so you can make strides toward your vision. It helps ensure that what you do matches up with what you have said you want to do. It may seem ridiculously simple, but putting accountability in place dramatically increases the chances of your following through. You've done your research, your idea is viable, you have a vision for where you'd like it to go, and perhaps you've even gotten some success under your belt. Now it's up to you to take it forward. Some people hear the word *accountability* and instantly feel like rebelling. They think of being forced to do things they don't want to do. They think of the times they have failed to finish something and, as a result, felt terribly disappointed in themselves. Or they think of someone standing over their shoulder making them feel badly about their lack of follow-through. But accountability doesn't have to call to mind Helga cracking a whip over your shoulder. (Helga is Lara's personal whip-cracker, in case you were wondering.) There are a variety of accountability techniques that don't involve whip-crackers named Helga, but if you go for that sort of thing, who are we to judge?

The good news here is that we want to help you stay accountable for things you actually want to do—the things that will get you where you want to go. We're going to say it again because it's one of the secrets that can get you to your version of success more quickly: if you want to move toward the vision of success you created in Chapter 2, make sure your to-do list is full of things that you actually want to do. This is not rocket science, but you might be surprised to know that many business owners think they have to do a bunch of things that they find awful. We aren't saying you'll love every minute of every day, but we do highly recommend finding a path that is appealing to you. After all, you are in charge of what your journey toward success looks like. *Phew.* Hopefully that makes you feel better and keeps your own version of Helga at bay. Keep in mind, this isn't a free pass to do only those things that are an absolute joy. (Bookkeeping always comes to mind here.) You will still need to follow through on tasks that aren't your favorite things to do. But here is where values and goals and vision come in: If you are able to link most of your to-dos with outcomes that are desirable, it will make them well worth doing. Let's review some of the different accountability techniques you can put to use.

Visual Reminders

Sometimes the simplest techniques can be powerfully effective. For example, a variety of visual reminders around your house, office, and car can go a long way toward keeping you on track. Consider a paper calendar on which you can track your day-to-day schedule as well as broken-out tasks for bigger projects. Lists (like the Hit Lists we introduced in previous chapters) are also a good way to keep track of what you need to do. Other ideas include a vision board for your grand plan, a Pinterest board dedicated to business ideas, a checklist of future milestones posted on the wall, and even sticky notes on your bulletin board or monitor for smaller tasks and reminders.

Tell a Friend

Let's say you have an idea that truly fires you up. You're committed to it because it matches up with your priorities and could potentially bring with it some rewards you're excited about. Here's something you might find compelling, which we've seen time and again with our clients: When you have an idea that inspires you, there is a small chance that you'll follow through on that idea. If you consciously commit to the idea, there is a slightly larger chance that you'll follow through. If you put a deadline in place, your chances for follow-through go up even more. If you tell someone about your idea and your deadline, your chances of actually doing it dramatically increase. And if you ask someone to check in with you on the due date, you are now highly likely to follow through. See how we're building in some accountability there?

All you have to do is set a deadline, tell someone about it, and ask him or her to check in with you about it. Voilà, it's as good as done. (Well, not really, as you have to actually do the thing you're setting out to do, but think of these as stepping stones to get you where you want to go.) Apparently, most of us don't like having to tell someone that we've neglected to do what we said we would do, so telling a friend about your plan can be a powerful motivator to get it done.

Appoint an Accountability Partner

An accountability partner takes the "tell a friend" idea a little further. Having an accountability partner is a fun way to connect with someone and make some leaps toward your vision at the same time. Ideally, you and your accountability partner are going through a shared experience, though that's not a requirement. Knowing that you and your partner are there to support each other can be just the push you need, to do the things you've committed to doing.

Work With a Coach or Mentor

Friends and accountability partners can be great, but sometimes you need the help of a pro. If connection with people is important to you, hiring a coach or working with a mentor may be your best bet. A coach or mentor becomes a trusted source to bounce ideas off of, one who can see things from an outside perspective and pushes you past your self-imposed limits. Again, knowing that someone will be checking in on you and expecting to hear about progress can be motivating. It can also affect your finances: According to *Success Magazine*'s April 2014 issue, business owners with a mentor were able to increase revenue an average of 106 percent versus 14 percent for those not receiving mentoring.[1] That makes for a pretty powerful argument in favor of having a mentor.

Moms Talk

Along this journey I figured out that I needed professional help. Not medical help (although that might have helped me get through a few of the rough days) but a business coach. I quickly discovered I didn't know as much as I thought I did. My business coach was a godsend and was critical in helping me organize the overwhelming list of tasks in a logical order, dealing with both the social isolation and the absence of a corporate structure to rely on. There is no right way or wrong way to approach entrepreneurship. My business coach helped me find my unique path and removed some of the sharp curves and speed bumps in the road.

　　—Veronica Mayo, Vemayca

As an entrepreneur, it's important for me to know why I am doing what I'm doing. It's not enough to say I want to start a project; I need to be clear with myself how each project is going to help me to reach my goals. I also take a look at what will happen when I complete the project, and what will happen if I don't. This "big why" is how I get things done and avoid procrastination. It's a way to hold myself accountable for completing the project.

　　—Kim Reddington, Cereus Women

Reward Yourself

May we also suggest that as you accomplish tasks and goals you mark them with some sort of celebration? Acknowledging a job well done is a smart way to encourage future action from yourself. These celebrations don't need to be time-consuming or expensive for you to get the benefit from them. One of our clients marks achievements by doing a happy dance. One lets herself have a delicious piece of dark chocolate that she saves just for these occasions. Lara gives herself a social media break and browses Facebook, Twitter, and Instagram for a few minutes. Be creative. The main point here is to pick something that will feel like a celebration. You deserve it. Creating this positive association will make you that much more motivated to keep going. Plus, if you plan well, you can check a self-care task off of your list at the same time. Refer back to that list of great self-care hacks we provided you in Chapter 4.

Here are some other tips that can help you get back on track:

- ✎ Find some inspiration in the form of quotes, books, movies, YouTube videos, and so on.
- ✎ Check in with your community and find some connection with others.
- ✎ Share your struggles and ask for specific help.
- ✎ Celebrate. It seems counterintuitive to celebrate when you are in a rut or feeling off track, but celebrating past accomplishments

or even the fact that you want to keep going when the going is hard is something to celebrate.

✎ Give, give, give. This one also seems counter-intuitive, but giving time or money to support someone else helps you zoom out and see the bigger picture.

✎ Get back to a good self-care routine.

✎ Look at the overall picture of your life. This can give you some much-needed perspective.

✎ Watch out for rules you've made up about what your journey as a mom business owner should look like. It may not look as you'd ex-pected it to look, and it may not look the way it looks for others, and that's okay.

✎ Go after low-hanging fruit. Accomplish a super-easy task to regain your momentum.

✎ Do the mindless tasks that often slip to the bottom of your to-do list but that drain a bit of your energy every time you realize you still haven't tackled them.

✎ Take care of your have-tos. These are the non-negotiables such as getting to the store for toilet paper or walking the dog before she has an accident in the house.

✎ Take a break—a fun, no-guilt-allowed break.

✎ Be gentle with yourself, nurture yourself, and let others care for you.

✎ Watch your self-talk and the *I can't*s we talked about in Chapter 4.

The Bigger Obstacles

Now that we've covered the minor obstacles, what about when things happen that make you wonder if it's time to give up altogether, or at least give up for now? There are certain life events that leave you with either a very difficult choice or no choice at all but to stop what you're doing so you can focus on the task at hand. Divorce, the death of someone close to you, a health diagnosis, a difficult pregnancy, or the termination of your partner's employment are examples of monumental life changes that can necessitate changing course quickly.

Erin faced this when she was diagnosed with a rare neurological disorder called Hemifacial Spasm (HFS). HFS causes the muscles on one side of your face to spasm to varying degrees. For Erin, it started out as a small eye twitch and progressed to the entire right side of her face. The spasms affected her self-esteem and her desire to go out in the world to grow her business. As a result, she actually shuttered her business for a year or so while she decided whether or not to go forward with the neurosurgery that had the potential to stop the spasming. She eventually had the surgery, and it was a success, which meant that she could get back to work coaching clients, speaking to moms' groups, and writing this book.

When these or other major life events happen, it's sometimes difficult to separate the emotion from the reality. This is especially true when the event sits squarely in the unwelcome news category. How do you know what to do about your business in these situations?

The answer can be surprisingly simple, and we recommend going back to the beginning of the book. Check in with your priorities. Have they suddenly shifted? If so, how does that change the time, effort, and energy you have to devote to the business? Does the event (or new circumstance) dramatically change your schedule? Check in with your intuition. What is still possible with your business in light of this new development? Check in with your self-care. Is it still possible to take good care of yourself, deal with the life event, and manage your business?

We can't answer these questions for you but we can tell you that sometimes major life events can send your business back to a previous stage (see Chapter 6) or spur you to come up with a Plan B. Can you scale way back for now? Can you put the business on hold? Are there employees you trust enough to put in charge for the time being? Can you try to sell the whole business? Or is it time to scale your company up, go full-time, and shift the dynamic and responsibilities on the home front so you can be the sole breadwinner?

In Chapter 5, we talked about some of the personality traits that can benefit your business. When you are facing a major life upheaval, perseverance, patience, courage, and confidence can really come into play. Call on your network and support system for helpful insight into the questions and challenges you are facing.

We should point out that it's not always unwelcome changes or something out of your control that causes you to shift your plans and priorities. Sometimes it's a realization on your part that you just want to do something different than what you've been doing. Our circumstances change. We change. And sometimes you just have to stop and true yourself up. That may mean going back to work full-time, scaling your business back, taking some time away from work altogether, or even revving up your business to the next level.

Moms Talk

Easing back on my consulting business and going back to work full-time wasn't an easy decision to make but it was a practical one. Business was slow and I found myself taking on small projects simply for the money. Our kids had just started school full-time, so it felt like the right time to start looking for a permanent, full-time position.

Today, I work for a university doing media relations, a role I am proud of and enjoy. While I miss being at home with my kids, the consistent income has been great and I feel like I'm on the right career path.

In the end, I wasn't able to let go of my business endeavor completely—I am too proud of the work I've done to build it—so I keep a short client list and do a little consulting work on the side. For me, it's the perfect balance of stability and entrepreneurship.

　　—Melissa Wenzel, Melissa Wenzel Communications

Because even the best-laid plans often get disrupted, it makes sense to think about how you'll handle the challenges that come your way. At some point, you will lose momentum, your children will get the flu, or your plans could shift significantly due to something you weren't expecting. These happenings will mean you either need to get back on track or potentially reevaluate your business altogether. We highly recommend spending a bit of time thinking about these things before they happen and having a plan in the back of your mind to deal with the obstacles, big or small. Do we sound like a broken record yet? Between our plans for just about everything and our encouragement to think about things in advance, you'd think we'd seen it turn out less than great for moms who didn't do these things. Oh, yes, we have seen that happen, and we want to help you avoid it.

Bottom Line

- ✎ It's not a matter of *if* something will throw you off track, it's a matter of *when.*
- ✎ Part of staying on track is planning and preparing for those times.

✎ A variety of accountability techniques are available. Choose the ones that will work for you.

✎ Sometimes a shift in your priorities (such as a major life change) will be the reason you get off track. Circle back to Chapter 1 to review your priorities and reevaluate your goals.

Conclusion

*I*f you've used this book to help you determine what you want and what's most important to you, if you've gleaned tidbits from successful business owners and acknowledged your strengths, and if you've gotten a better handle on how best to spend your time and now have a plan for how to move forward—congratulations! You're well on your way to creating a successful company and a happy life.

By completing the exercises in this book, you are doing the necessary inner work and matching it to business planning and strategy work to create a life that fulfills you. Rather than following someone else's path, you are creating your own. This path might seem more difficult at first, but by *truing up* at each step along the way, the business you create will be well integrated with your life. You won't have to worry about them being at odds with each other because you will have created a business and a life that fit together like the puzzle pieces they are.

We'll leave you with one other thing to remember—but at least this one should come naturally to you. Being authentically you in business is definitely the way to go. A huge part of your potential success as a mom entrepreneur has to do with being true to yourself. Sure, people suggest that you should "fake it until you make it," and there is sometimes value in putting on an air of confidence in business dealings. However, if you've never seen Simon Sinek's TEDTalk, go watch it now. It's about how great leaders inspire action, but all of what he says is relevant to you as a business owner. Being genuine helps you attract the right clients and customers. It helps you move toward a success that reflects you, and it keeps you on the right track as you navigate everything that owning a business can throw your way. It's also your best bet for living a life that feels happy.

Starting something is usually the hardest part, and guess what? By using this book, you've already gotten started in a powerful way. Doing the exercises throughout this book put you well ahead of many other entrepreneurs. And, because you've created the foundation and started building a lifestyle that honors your priorities and has you doing work that fulfills you, you're going to create a path that will work well for you. Yay, you! You are taking the time now to put the odds in your favor by purposefully choosing what works for you—and what doesn't.

One last thought: We highly recommend scheduling check-ins with yourself every three to six months. Just as your family and business continue to grow and evolve, so will your plans. Look back over your priorities. Review your values. Adjust your schedule as needed. None of these things are set in stone, so feel free to make changes and then double-check that what you are doing—both in business and in life—still matches up with what's most important to you. Revisiting the exercises and information in this book will provide insight for years to come, so go ahead and put this book on your bookshelf once you've completed it—but we'd highly recommend choosing a shelf that's easy to access.

You'll know that you are on the right track if you feel confident and empowered and excited and capable. The sooner you start, the sooner you'll see the results of your hard work, so get to it.

Notes

Introduction

1. Fitzgerald, Michael. "Women Make Better Managers Than Men." *www.cbsnews.com/news/women-make-better-managers-than-men/*

2. Zenger, Jack and Joseph Folkman. "Are Women Better Leaders Than Men?" *http://blogs.hbr.org/2012/03/a-study-in-leadership-women-do/*

Chapter 3

1. Vanderkam, Laura. *168 Hours: You Have More Time Than You Think.* Portfolio Hardcover, 2010.

2. Loehr, Jim, and Tony Schwartz. *The Power of Full Engagement.* Free Press, 2005.

Chapter 4

1. Konigsberg, Ruth Davis. "Time Management Techniques for the Modern Woman." *Real Simple* online: *www.realsimple.com/work-life/ life-strategies/time-management/time-man- agement-techniques-00100000077227/index. html.*

Chapter 5

1. Rath, Tom. *Strengthsfinder 2.0.* New York: Gallup Press, 2007.

2. Hanford, Emily. "Angela Duckworth and the Research on 'Grit.'" American Public Media: American Radio Works online: *http://ameri- canradioworks.publicradio.org/features/tomor- rows-college/grit/angela-duckworth-grit.html.*

3. Mayo Center Staff. "Social Support: Tap this tool to beat stress." *www.mayoclinic.org/ healthy-living/stress-management/in-depth/ social-support/art-20044445*

Chapter 6

1. The series includes the following books, all published by Jim Horan's The One Page Business Plan Company: *The One-Page Business Plan for the Creative Entrepreneur* (2004), *The One-Page Business Plan for the Professional Consultant* (2006), *The One-Page Business Plan for Non-Profit Organizations* (2007), *The One-Page Business Plan for the Busy Executive*, *The One-Page Business Plan for Financial Services Professionals*, and *The One-Page Business Plan for Women in Business.*

Chapter 7

1. Fowler, Page. "Talk Yourself Into (or Out Of) Just About Anything. *www.lhj.com/health/ news/talk-yourself-into-anything/*

Chapter 8

1. SUCCESS staff. "The Perks of Getting a Mentor." *www.success.com/article/ the-perks-of-getting-a-mentor*

Appendix A

22 Things You Can Outsource to a Virtual Assistant

Virtual assistants (VAs) provide a variety of services and specializations. Here are some examples of how they can help:

1. Data entry
2. Document preparation and transcription
3. Typing, editing, and proofreading
4. Creating and sending out newsletters or e-zines
5. Accounting
6. Bookkeeping
7. Preparation of financial documents
8. Customer service support by e-mail or phone
9. Monitoring and prioritizing your e-mails

10. Responding to e-mails on your behalf

11. Designing, updating, and managing Websites and blogs

12. Setting up accounts on social networking sites like LinkedIn, Twitter, and Facebook

13. Managing your online social networking accounts

14. Copywriting (web copy, press releases, sales letters, and other materials)

15. Product development research

16. Market research

17. Calendar management

18. Contact management

19. Bulk mailings

20. Meeting and event arrangements

21. Travel arrangements

22. Document and image scanning

Appendix B

List of Contributors

Amy Anderson, Fleurish Partners
www.fleurishpartners.com

Lara Anderson, RD Shady
www.rdshady.com

Andreea Ayers, Launch Grow Joy
www.launchgrowjoy.com

Traci Bartee, Fly Fitness
www.wearesuperfly.com

Veronica Bosgraaf, PURE Bar
www.thepurebar.com

Kathryn Cree Bouchard, tweak
www.tweakitsimple.com

Kathy Buckworth
www.kathybuckworth.com

Michal Chesal, Baby K'tan
www.babyktan.com

Michelle Ciarlo-Hayes, MKC Photography
www.mkcphotography.com

Julie Cole, Mabel's Labels
www.mabelslabels.com

Susan Slater Cotter, STRENGTHstudio
www.strength-studio.com

Karen Czarnik, Super Blanky™
www.superblanky.com

Michelle Dale, Virtual Miss Friday
www.michelle-dale.com

Erin Dullea, 52 Dares
www.52dares.com

Jacqueline Ernst
www.ernstconnected.com

Elayna Fernandez, The Positive Mom
www.thepositivemom.com

Julie Fry, Business Among Moms
www.businessamongmoms.com

Debra Gano, *BYOU (Be Your Own You) Magazine*
www.byoumagazine.com

Hilary Genga, Trunkettes
www.trunkettes.com

Terry Grahl, Enchanted Makeovers
www.enchantedmakeovers.org

Holly Hanna, The Work at Home Woman
www.theworkathomewoman.com

Becky Harper, ReUsies
www.reusies.com

Cause Haun, See Kai Run
www.seekairun.com

Sarah Kirk, Swoop Bags
www.swoopbags.com

Sharelle Klaus, Dry Soda
www.drysoda.com

Carley Knobloch, Carley K
www.carleyk.com

Kristy Lewis, Quinn Popcorn
www.quinnpopcorn.com

Naomi Lewis, High Maintenance Skincare Studio
www.highmaintenanceskin.com

Veronica Mayo, Vemayca
www.vemayca.com

Michelle McCullough, Startup Princess
www.startupprincess.com

Britt Menzies, StinkyKids
www.stinkykids.com

Lisa Merriam, Merriam Associates
www.merriamassociates.com

Rikki Mor, Knot Genie
www.knotgenie.com

Sue Anne Morgan, ideaLand
www.idealand.com

Trish Morrison, MomCom
www.momcomlife.com

Kelsey Ramsden
www.kelseyramsden.ca

Kim Reddington, Cereus Women
www.cereuswomen.com

Kea Rensh, Merin Designs
www.merindesigns.com

Gabby Roffey, tweak
www.tweakitsimple.com

Jill Salzman, The Founding Moms
www.foundingmoms.com

Margie Scherschligt, Margie Photo
www.margie.scherschligt.com

Dr. Elaine Fogel Schneider, Touch Time International
www.touchtime.org

Pat Stone, Bell Stone Toffee
www.bellstonetoffee.com

Cathy Tousley, Furlesse
www.furlesse.com

Kim Walls, Episencial
www.episencial.com

Grace Welch, patemm inc.
www.patemm.com

Melissa Wenzel, Melissa Wenzel Communications

Karen Whorton, ReUsies
www.reusies.com

Shannon Wilburn, Just Between Friends
www.jbfsale.com

Appendix C

Author Q&A

How did you two meet?

Erin: Well, we were introduced via a colleague. We hadn't actually met in person until after we wrote the book. We were able to throw out the rule about needing to be in the same state as your coauthor.

Lara: In my quest to surround myself with women smarter than myself, I started a mastermind group for life coaches in 2009, and luckily we had a colleague in common who suggested Erin join the group. I was living in Ontario, Canada, at the time and feeling pretty isolated from my family and friends back in the States, so being able to connect with women like Erin, regardless of where we were all located, was a lifeline for me.

Describe your partnership.

E: It's been an amazing partnership—almost too good to be true, really. We have some different skills and some that overlap. Lara has some strengths that have contributed greatly to the success of our partnership, and, besides that, I just really like her. That's always a huge plus when you are going to work with someone on a huge project.

L: Let's see... Fun? Simpatico? Kinda nirvana? I've been in a lot of relationships and partnerships in my life, and some are examples of opposites attracting the other or strengths and weaknesses balancing each other out. But my partnership with Erin is more "like meets like." Our personalities and strengths help maximize the other. If one of us starts something, the other finishes it. Or we both do the same thing at the same time. In a word, our partnership is easy.

How do you approach work/life balance?

E: I think we both bristle a bit at the phrase *work/life balance*, though I appreciate when I feel as though things in my life are balanced. I always say that there is no perfect balance—you are either moving toward it or you are moving away from it. I know when I'm moving away from it because I get crabby and resentful. That's my clue to spend more time in whatever areas I've been neglecting.

L: Do the things that matter the most to you. Let go of the things that don't matter much to you. Sounds simple, but Erin and I both have a built a career out of helping other women live by this guide. It's not simple because we often have conflicting priorities and a high bar for how we do everything in our lives.

What's your advice to other moms who want to own their own businesses?

E: Do it! Find something you want to do and then make a plan to do it—using our book, of course! We need more women business owners. We need more women pursuing work (in whatever form) that makes them happy. I know it's not always possible, but taking small steps in that direction can go a long way toward creating a successful business once it is the right time in your life to pursue that.

L: Although it's probably easier to make money working for someone else, being your own boss is the ticket to having the freedom, flexibility, and fulfillment through your work that moms like us crave. Being a business owner is satisfying on so many levels. You get to model for your kids what it looks like to have a dream and follow it. You get the opportunity to test yourself and grow in ways you just wouldn't otherwise. Just be willing to ask for help—at home and in your business.

What have you learned that you wish you had known earlier?

E: I've learned to take risks. I've learned to care less about what others think of me. I've learned that my kids will survive if they have to eat cereal for dinner every now and then. I've learned to show up as me without apology. And I've learned that asking and hearing no for an answer is better than not asking at all.

L: I own my time. Period. If I could go back to my 30-year-old self who was leaving her career in corporate America to stay home and raise her first child, I would pour her a strong cup of coffee, look her in the eye and tell her this: "No matter how many times you hear the kids calling you from the other room, no matter how insistently your husband reminds you there are no clean socks in the house, and no matter how urgently you think you have to respond to that prospect's inquiry about hiring you, *you are the boss of your time.*" I spent way too much time feeling like a victim to how much everybody else needed me. I thought, *I could get things done if only everybody (including my babies) would just let me be!* Once I learned to organize my time and spend it on my priorities, I stopped feeling so stressed out and overwhelmed. I set boundaries, make plans, and finally feel satisfied with what I accomplish (most of the time).

What's the best part about owning your own business while being a mother?

E: For me, the best part is the independence I have. I set my own schedule so I can volunteer or attend an event at my kids' schools. I am home when the kids get home from school. And I really do feel like I'm showing them that a career can look how you want it to look. There are definitely things I'm giving up by choosing this path—steady income, health benefits, and paid vacation come to mind—but I wouldn't willingly trade the flexibility, autonomy, and sense of fulfillment I get in exchange.

L: Ditto for me what Erin said. But there's also this huge feeling of accomplishment when I look at my company and realize that I created it from scratch. It's mine. I am proud of what I've been able to do and especially the ability to help other mom entrepreneurs do the same for themselves.

What's the hardest part?

E: Being responsible for everything. I'm responsible for the growth (or lack thereof) of my company. I'm responsible for getting clients. I'm responsible for marketing and social media and taxes. The other hardest part is that I have more ideas than I could ever act on.

L: I struggle with managing the day-to-day operations. I like to do things when the inspiration hits me, like blogging, shooting a video, calling and checking in on a current or past client, or making a connection with a potential collaboration partner. But the fact is that running a business takes a lot of discipline to do things according to a schedule, a plan, or your calendar. Fortunately, I know my limits and have expanded my team to include a business partner, a business manager, and virtual assistants that help me keep the balls in the air and the projects on track. Without them, I doubt I'd still be in business.

What's next for you?

E: I hope what's next is more writing and more work with women who want to take the leap into owning their own business. I absolutely love working with women one on one but I also think it's time to offer some group work to maximize my time and to make coaching more affordable to all women.

L: I definitely want to write more books with Erin! And in my own career as a coach and speaker, I'm committed to spreading the messages we teach in our book on a much larger scale. I'll be doing a lot more speaking at conferences and to women's and small business organizations, and I'd love to become a regular contributor on national radio and TV shows.

Index

About the Authors

Erin Baebler has spent the past 10 years providing coaching to women in transition through her company, Magnolia Workshop. She published an essay in *Chicken Soup for the Soul: New Moms* and was a contributor to *Five Must-Know Secrets for Today's College Girl*. Erin is a sought-after speaker for Seattle-area moms' groups. She can be found on the Web at *www.magnoliaworkshop.com*, on Facebook at Magnolia Workshop, or on Twitter at @magnoliawkshop.

Lara Galloway, the Mom Biz Coach, is a speaker, business coach, and mentor to mom entrepreneurs and small business owners. Her passion is helping entrepreneurs create and run businesses that honor their priorities and values. She is the founder of MomBizCoach, the host of the MomBiz Solutions Show weekly podcast, and co-founder of MomBiz, MommyCoach, and the Founding Moms of Metro Detroit Meetup. If it has something to do with moms and entrepreneurship, you'll find her in the middle of it, or quite possibly leading it.

Lara is frequently featured for her expertise on work/life balance, starting and running a successful small business, marketing your business on social media, and creatively managing your time in media like *Forbes*, *Crain's Business*, *the Chicago Tribune*, and *More Magazine*. She has been highlighted on multiple mom entrepreneur "top" lists, including Top 50 Mompreneur Blogs 2013 (*Mompreneur Media*), Top 30 Women Entrepreneurs to Follow on Twitter (*Forbes*), and 100 Most Powerful Women on Twitter (Hubspot). In addition, Lara (@mombizcoach) has more than 25,000 Twitter followers and a podcast that averages 4,000 downloads each week.

For more information:

Website: *www.MomsMeanBusinessBook.com*

Twitter: @MomsMeanBiz

Facebook: MomsMeanBusiness